I0782404

NUCLEAR WAR SURVIVAL MANUAL PART II

Mastering Survival Techniques for Nuclear Fallout, Attacks, and EMP Threats – A Comprehensive Pocket Guide 2024

Prabal Jain

RC Publishers

RC PUBLISHERS

Copyright © 2024 Prabal Jain

All rights reserved

The characters and events portrayed in this book are fictitious. Any similarity to real persons, living or dead, is coincidental and not intended by the author.

No part of this book may be reproduced, or stored in a retrieval system, or transmitted in any form or by any means, electronic, mechanical, photocopying, recording, or otherwise, without express written permission of the publisher.

ISBN: 9798324789374
Imprint: Independently published

CONTENTS

INTRODUCTION

*Recap: A Forced Farewell and the
Journey Through the Mountains*

Days 301-304 saw significant changes for me. Having been ousted from the only safe haven I knew due to my dishonesty about my past, I had to leave without a word to my friends Alexis, Lilith, Annie, Meg, or Robbie. The necessity for their safety outweighed my desire to have them by my side, especially since I had learned of a new threat—a group forming an army in the desert, attempting to claim their stake in what's left of the United States.

With the government bunkered down and the land being ravaged by nuclear warfare, chaos reigned outside the small bubbles of civilization like the town I was forced to leave. Following a tip from a Raider, I set out alone, tracing their path through the mountains in hopes of learning more about this emerging army.

Days 305-309 were challenging. The mountains were treacherous, covered in thick snow and ash from the nuclear fallout. I traveled through service roads and highways, always wearing breathing protection to shield myself from the radioactive particles. My pace was faster alone, allowing me to close in on the Raiders who had survived a previous attack and fled their camp. Unfortunately, I stumbled upon a grim scene— a campsite where survivors had stayed, and among them, a man who had met a brutal end, likely at the hands of cannibals.

As I continued my pursuit, the uncertainty of what I'd face once I reached the Raiders and their new leader loomed over me. Yet, I knew that gathering intelligence was crucial. What I would decide to do with that information remained to be seen, but for now, my focus was clear: follow the trail, stay safe, and prepare for whatever awaited me at the end of this journey.

CHAPTER 1: CLOSING IN AND STRIKING STEALTHILY

Days 310-313 were marked by determination as I saw the Raider's campfire glowing in the distance at night. Their lack of caution made them easy to spot, and each day, I pushed myself a bit harder to shorten the distance between us. Knowing there were about five or six Raiders, plus any new recruits they might have gathered, I had to be cautious. Too much haste could lead to exhaustion, and I needed to be fully prepared for the confrontation that was inevitable.

The captives were always on my mind. The Raiders had taken people from their previous raids, and with their ruthless actions at the last campsite, I knew these hostages were in great danger. The thought of what happened to the man they killed fueled my urgency, but I had to approach this carefully.

Days 314-315, I shifted my strategy to nighttime movements. Under the cover of darkness, I crept closer to their camp. The Raiders had set up a lax security with only two guards on the night watch. Tied to a tree, I spotted two women, one likely in her forties and a younger one, possibly a teenager. The man I had found dead must have been their father.

In total, there were seven Raiders; five were asleep while the two guards watched over the captives and their supplies. The guards weren't very vigilant, chatting and joking, unaware that I had tracked them down from Big Bear.

Taking advantage of their carelessness, I decided to thin their numbers quietly before making a major move. The chilling cold bit into my bones as I waited for the right moment. Finally, one guard joked about needing a break and walked away from the camp. I followed him silently until he stopped behind a bush. He didn't notice my approach, and my knife found its mark quietly in the dark. This silent takedown was just the beginning of my plan to dismantle their hold and rescue the captives.

A Nighttime Assault and Tactical Escalation

On the second night after observing the Raider's camp, I decided it was time to make a more decisive move. I had eliminated one guard quietly the previous night, and I was determined not to alert the entire camp with a hasty rescue. I needed a strategic approach, especially since I couldn't risk the safety of the captives by involving them directly in a potential firefight.

As I approached the camp under the cover of night, the freshly fallen snow muffled my footsteps, aiding my stealth. The two guards on duty were noticeably more vigilant than the previous ones, likely spooked by the disappearance of their comrade. I crept within 30 feet of the tents, where I paused, raised my M4 rifle, and took aim. With just four quick pulls of the trigger, both guards were down.

The noise, however, stirred the others inside the tents, who scrambled for their weapons. Seizing the moment, I used a piece of old weaponry I had acquired from the Raiders at

Big Bear—a Vietnam-era fragmentation grenade, likely from a raided National Guard Armory. I threw the grenade towards the entrance of one of the tents just as its flap was being torn open. The explosion was immediate and devastating, not lethal to all inside, but enough to severely incapacitate anyone left.

With half of their force either down or disoriented, I turned my attention to the second tent. The survivors were disorganized and slow, making them easy targets as they tried to exit the chaos. I was grateful for having traded my hunting rifle for the M4, which offered me the rapid response capability I needed in this critical moment.

This tactical approach significantly reduced the threat level, allowing me to focus on securing the safety of the captives without the risk of a full-scale retaliation from the Raiders.

A New Mission with Clara and Alana

As the conflict at the Raider's camp settled, I approached the captives. The first tent echoed with the moans of the wounded. With my knife in hand, I quickly moved to where Clara and her teenage daughter, Alana, were still tied to a tree. I cut their ropes and instructed them to follow me quietly into the darkness, away from the camp. Although I was hesitant to leave the wounded Raiders, I knew they wouldn't survive the night, allowing us to escape without further confrontation.

Days 316-320 were filled with decisions. Clara and Alana, still shaken by their ordeal and the brutal loss of their husband and father, were not in a condition to travel alone. My initial plan had been to continue pursuing the Raider's army, but the immediate needs of Clara and Alana took precedence. Instead of sending them back toward Big Bear, where they came from, I chose to guide them west, towards a small, welcoming community in the desert that I knew about.

Using my map, I found a road that could lead us out of the mountains and into the desert. The journey was challenging, as the roads were no longer maintained and covered with snow, making our hike particularly difficult.

Days 321-324 brought insights into Clara and Alana's backstory. They had fled from north of Los Angeles after the nuclear bombs fell. Like many in Southern California, their community depended heavily on electricity for water supply. Once the power grid was destroyed, their water supply stopped, forcing them and many others to migrate. While many headed north hoping to escape further bombings in rural Northern California, others moved east towards the Heartland. Our journey through the snow-laden paths was slow but determined, as I led them towards a place of safety and a new beginning.

Challenges and Compassion on the Journey

As we moved further south, the topic of our conversations often revolved around how life had changed since the collapse of civilization. We talked in a way that many who have experienced trauma might understand—skirting around the deepest sorrows and focusing instead on vague reminisces like "I used to do this" or "I used to do that." There was an unspoken pact among survivors not to dredge up the painful past or the loved ones we had lost.

During our discussions, we touched on the stark transformations in human behavior in this new world. I shared a poignant quote I remembered, which suggested that civilization survives only a few minutes after the power goes out. It had been over 320 days since the disaster, and here we were, evidence of that grim reality, as I followed leads on an army that was trying to claim a part of Southern California.

Days 325-329 brought a new challenge. Alana twisted her ankle, resulting in a severe limp. The fear in her eyes was palpable; she was terrified that her injury would slow us down too much. I could tell she was worried that I might decide to leave her and her mother behind because of this setback. This fear gave me a chill—it was a stark reminder of the distrust that had taken root in our world.

Clara quickly took charge, wrapping Alana's ankle and helping her to manage the pain. Meanwhile, I busied myself with making a splint from the surrounding trees. We were a team, and I was determined to show Alana and Clara that despite the harshness of our reality, we wouldn't abandon each other. We continued our journey, adjusting our pace to accommodate Alana's injury, reinforcing our mutual commitment to stick together no matter the challenges ahead.

Reassurances and a New Encounter

As we continued our challenging descent through the snowy and ashy mountains, I took the time to craft a makeshift crutch for Alana from branches. Despite my assurances, Clara seemed skeptical about my commitment to their safety. She repeatedly emphasized her medical skills, possibly thinking that by highlighting her usefulness, she would ensure their continued inclusion in my plans.

One night, I pulled Clara aside to reassure her explicitly. I told her that their safety was my priority, and I had no intentions of abandoning them. Her skills as a nurse, while invaluable, were not the condition of my support. I was committed to them out of principle, not utility. This conversation seemed to relieve a great burden from Clara, leading to an emotional moment where she broke down and embraced me, releasing pent-up tears.

Back at our campfire, Clara composed herself, putting on a brave face for Alana. We pushed forward, our pace slowed by Alana's injury but aided by the supplies we had scavenged from the Raiders. After a week of careful travel, we noticed a thin stream of smoke rising from a fire somewhere down a dirt road. Concerned about potential dangers, I instructed Clara and Alana to stay hidden while I investigated.

Approaching cautiously, I found a small cabin with smoke issuing from its chimney. As I circled the cabin for a better view through the windows, I was suddenly stopped by the sound of a safety being flicked off. A deep, gravelly voice broke the silence, challenging my presence near their hideout.

An Unexpected Ally in the Wilderness

As I faced the business end of a shotgun, the man holding it looked every bit the hardened survivor. His life on the fringes of civilization likely meant the chaos of the world's end barely altered his daily reality. He demanded to know who I was and how many were with me. I answered honestly, explaining it was just me and two others seeking safety.

His suspicious gaze didn't waver as I spoke. In this new, brutal world, trust was a rare commodity. However, I could tell he wasn't aligned with the cannibals roaming the mountains; the evidence was in the animal skins drying on his rack, a sign he hunted wildlife, not humans.

He listened intently as I recounted our escape from the city, our brief time at the community by the Salton Sea, and our encounter with the Raiders at Big Bear. His next question caught me off guard: "How many people have you killed?" I replied truthfully, only as many as necessary to protect those under my care. He seemed to accept this, his posture relaxing slightly as the shotgun lowered.

He then motioned for me to follow him into the cabin, where he disarmed me. Though I was uneasy, I had little choice but to comply. Inside, he quickly grabbed a pair of crutches, better suited for Alana than the makeshift one I had created. As we left his cabin, he issued a stern warning, "If you're lying, you're as good as dead." His straightforwardness was oddly reassuring.

With the shotgun no longer aimed at me but still present, I led him to where Clara and Alana were hiding. At first, their alarm was visible, but as the old man noticed their fear, his demeanor softened. He lowered his shotgun, almost apologetically, and his expression shifted to one of regret. "No, no, I'm sorry, ladies," he began, a rare glimpse of remorse in his rugged features.

A Change of Heart

Watson introduced himself properly and provided Alana with the crutches, making her mobility much easier. He then extended an invitation for us to stay at his cabin for the night. Days 334-339 turned into a few days' stay as we allowed Alana's ankle to heal, a decision Watson insisted on. During our time there, I realized that Watson was a complex character: outwardly tough, but with a surprisingly gentle core. This contrast reminded me of Alexis, stirring a painful memory that I quickly suppressed.

In conversations, Watson shared his concerns about Raiders and scavengers in the mountains. He had been monitoring and discouraging any groups that trespassed on what he considered his land. His ability to move silently was impressive; he had managed to approach me undetected, which was no small feat.

While enjoying the real meat he provided, we discussed the decreasing game in the area, a problem both he and the folks at Big Bear were experiencing. We hoped it was a temporary shift in the wildlife patterns due to the new world conditions.

Then, unexpectedly, Alana invited Watson to join us on our journey. "You can't stay locked up in these mountains forever, especially with the game running out," she said earnestly. Watson's initial reaction was one of discomfort; living alone had been his way for so long that the idea of joining a group was clearly unsettling.

However, as we pressed the idea that we could benefit from his help, I witnessed a remarkable change in him. The tough, solitary mountain man seemed to soften under Alana's earnest appeal. His usual stern demeanor gave way, and he visibly flushed with emotion. It was clear that beneath his rugged exterior, Watson harbored a deep capacity for connection. Alana had touched a soft spot in him, and it seemed he was seriously considering our proposal to come with us.

Journey Through the Desert

By the time Alana could put weight on her foot again, we were ready to resume our journey. Each day spent idle heightened my anxiety, as the threat to Big Bear loomed larger with the potential of a growing enemy army. I was burdened with questions about this army's size, leadership, and intentions—especially whether they might attack Big Bear again or target another area. Despite these uncertainties, my priority remained fulfilling the promise I made to ensure Alana and her mother's safety.

To my relief and slight surprise, Watson decided to join us. His interactions with Alana hinted at a past connection, possibly with a daughter of his own, but I respected his privacy and didn't press the matter. Having Watson with us was a boon. His expertise as a tracker and woodsman was invaluable, and his presence seemed to speed our progress.

With Watson guiding us, we were able to navigate more efficiently. His knowledge of the land helped us find quicker paths, and soon we were moving out of the mountainous region and into the desert. Our destination lay southwest, and with the mountains and snow behind us, we estimated it would only take a few more days on foot.

Days 346 to 350 saw us taking a cautious approach to our travel. We chose a route that skirted the western shore of the lake, deliberately avoiding Slab City and any potential conflicts there. This detour, though longer, provided us with a safer passage and allowed us to manage our resources and energy more effectively as we neared our goal. The landscape changed, and the challenges of the desert terrain tested our resilience, but with Watson's guidance and the group's renewed strength, we pushed forward towards our destination.

Confronting Danger

During our journey, we took advantage of the abandoned buildings along the Salton Sea's perimeter for shelter at night. These structures provided a sense of security, although we remained vigilant, especially near Slab City—a place notorious for its lawless drifters and now, a hub for Raiders.

We kept our presence discreet, avoiding fires and eating our meals cold to stay under the radar. One night, Watson felt uneasy, suspecting we were being watched. Trusting his instincts, he disappeared into the desert, moving with the stealth and precision of a panther.

At dawn, Watson returned with a man in tow, dressed in tattered travel clothes with his hands bound. He threw the man into our temporary shelter and expressed his frustration with a spit on the ground. This man, a scout, had been lurking nearby, confirming Watson's suspicions.

The scout, under the stern gaze of Watson's shotgun, hurled insults until a swift hit from the butt of the gun silenced him. With the weapon now pointed squarely at him, he became cooperative. Through our interrogation, a chilling picture emerged: he was part of a smaller group of Raiders scouting the area around the Salton Sea, specifically targeting the farms we were headed towards. They planned to raid these farms soon, a thought that sent a cold shiver down my spine, considering the potential danger to the unsuspecting community.

After we had gathered all the necessary information, Clara, concerned for the scout's fate, asked what we would do with him. Watson, ever the pragmatist, took it upon himself to manage the situation. He assured us he would deal with the scout and advised us to move ahead. His decision left us with mixed feelings, but we trusted his judgment and prepared to continue our journey, wary of the looming threat and fortified by the knowledge we had gained.

A Warm Return to the Farms

Upon returning to the farms after months away, I was struck by the transformation. Under Ruslana's governance, the community had taken significant strides in fortifying its perimeter. The fence, though still under construction, had sections reinforced with concrete barriers, indicating they had access to a fuel depot and stabilizers—key for operating machinery since gasoline degrades quickly.

As we approached, the presence of new guard towers underscored the community's vigilance. We were spotted well before reaching the gates, and a group of riflemen came out to meet us. Their caution was understandable, given the ongoing threats from Raiders and other malign forces in the area.

The reception from the patrol was warm, particularly from those who recognized me. There was an outpouring of camaraderie with backslapping and eager inquiries about our journey and wellbeing. I decided to hold off on sharing our news until we were fully inside and could inform everyone together.

Once inside, Ruslana, having been alerted by radio of our arrival, was there to welcome us. Her leadership had clearly steered the community through challenging times, and her presence was reassuring. The sense of order and progress within the farms was palpable, offering a stark contrast to the lawlessness we had navigated to get here. It was a moment of relief and renewed hope as we stepped into the relative safety and structure of the community, ready to share our experiences and the intelligence we had gathered on potential threats.

Settling in at Farm Bridge

Upon my return to the farms, now officially named Farm Bridge, the reunion with Ruslana was both warm and fraught with concern. She was immediately inquisitive about the safety of the girls and Robbie, and I briefed her on the recent attack at Big Bear and the ongoing threats we had encountered. Ruslana's reaction was grave; she and her community had been aware of the rumors about a gathering army and had experienced their own problems with raiders from Slab City, which justified the newly erected fences and guard towers.

Days 356 to 360 were a period of much-needed respite. Farm Bridge offered comforts that seemed almost luxurious after our arduous journey, including the ability to take a warm shower —a small pleasure that felt extraordinarily rejuvenating. While part of my mind lingered on Alexis and others I missed, I forced myself to focus on the present.

Ruslana and I spent considerable time strategizing on how to bolster the community's defenses and support its growth. Farm Bridge had become a sanctuary, slowly expanding as more survivors from the cities joined us. The community's name reflected its aspirations: 'Farm' illustrated its agricultural basis and 'Bridge' symbolized hope for a bridge to a brighter future. This place had become a critical hub in Southern California, attracting not just new residents but also unwanted attention from raiders.

The strategic importance of Farm Bridge was underscored by continuous threats. Despite successfully repelling two major attacks from Slab City, the community remained vigilant, regularly intercepting scouts in the surrounding hills. Our discussions were abruptly interrupted with alarming news: a convoy tasked with bringing in more survivors and supplies had been ambushed. This new threat required immediate attention and planning, highlighting the ongoing challenges we faced in safeguarding this burgeoning beacon of hope.

Tracking the Raiders

Days 361-365 were spent tracing the Raiders who had attacked the convoy. Ruslana, with her military background, initially wanted to lead the response, but she conceded to letting Watson and me take charge of the tracking due to our specialized skills. We set off towards the site of the ambush, moving as quickly as possible through the rugged desert terrain.

The scene at the attack site was grim. The Raiders had thoroughly scavenged the convoy's makeshift wagons, which had been ingeniously built atop old car chassis by the engineers at Farm Bridge. The assault wasn't just a robbery; it was a devastating blow to our logistics and morale. We found several bodies—both survivors of the convoy and Raiders. Fortunately, these Raiders, likely from Slab City, weren't cannibals; they hadn't resorted to butchering the bodies. However, the survivors captured would likely be sold into slavery, potentially even to cannibals, adding urgency to our mission.

Days 366 to 368 involved following the Raiders' tracks northward, paralleling the coastline of the Salton Sea. It appeared the slavers were deliberately avoiding Farm Bridge by taking a longer route around the vast inland lake. This detour suggested they were cautious of our community's defenses, yet it provided us with a clearer trail to follow. As we tracked them, the stakes were high, and every moment counted to catch up to the slavers and attempt a rescue of the captured survivors.

Stealth Mission at Slab City

Days 369-372 took us to the outskirts of Slab City, near the iconic Salvation Mountain. This massive, brightly painted hill stood out starkly against the desert backdrop. Despite its colors fading from neglect, the landmark served as a useful navigation point as we entered what was technically the outer perimeter of Slab City. We proceeded with extreme caution, opting to move only under the cover of night to avoid detection, given our limited numbers and the high stakes.

Ruslana was wary of escalating to a full-scale conflict with Slab City. It was clear from her tense expression that she anticipated future confrontations, but hoped they could be avoided until we were better prepared. Our immediate concern was the disorganized nature of Slab City's slavers, who lacked a unified command, making them less effective as a cohesive force. This disarray could work to our advantage.

Watson and I conducted reconnaissance under the darkness, splitting up to cover more ground around the settlement. We discovered that the slavers didn't have a central holding area for captives. Instead, they were divided into smaller groups, each managing its own separate enclosures for prisoners. This decentralization was a piece of fortunate news for us. It suggested that we might be able to stage multiple small-scale rescues, simulating a series of unrelated prison breaks.

Our strategy was crucial; we needed to ensure that these actions did not appear as a coordinated effort from Farm Bridge. If the slavers suspected that the rescues were organized by our community, it could provoke a vendetta against us. Although Slab City's inhabitants typically struggled with cooperation, a direct threat to their operations might unify them against Farm Bridge, a risk we were not prepared to face just yet.

The Raid on Slab City

During days 373 to 375, we executed our plan to infiltrate the northern skirts of Slab City, aiming for a swift and stealthy rescue operation. The open desert terrain offered little cover, complicating our approach. We couldn't sneak up as close as we preferred, so we opted for a more direct assault.

Two of Ruslana's sharpshooters positioned themselves on small rises several hundred meters away in the desert, providing them with a clear line of sight. The rest of us used a dry riverbed (wadi) to advance undetected as close as possible to the slavers' encampment. We managed to get within about a hundred meters of the structures where about a dozen slaves were stationed, with the nearest backup group half a mile away.

On Ruslana's signal, the operation commenced. The quiet of the night was shattered by the synchronized shots of our sharpshooters. As two slavers fell instantly, we surged forward. However, an unforeseen third slaver, likely disturbed from sleep, appeared from behind a stack of tires and aimed his rifle at us. Quick action from one of Ruslana's team took him down before he could fire.

With no time to tend to wounds or mourn any losses, we pressed on. I used the remaining grenades to create a diversion and disrupt any further resistance. As I lobbed a grenade towards one of the structures, Ruslana worked swiftly on the lock to the captives' pen.

In a stroke of either luck or misfortune, a slaver ran out just as the grenade exploded, effectively removing another threat. The chaos provided us with a critical window to break open the pen and start extracting the captives, each moment filled with intense urgency to save as many lives as possible.

Escape from Slab City

During days 376-380, we pushed ourselves to the limit, rapidly increasing our distance from Slab City. The successful extraction of the captives was tinged with tension, as we anticipated pursuit from the slavers. However, surprisingly, no chase ensued. This unexpected lack of retaliation left us uneasy; it was unusual for a group like the Slab City slavers to not retaliate, especially after such a direct assault on their territory.

Watson and I shared a look of mutual suspicion. The absence

of pursuit could mean we had eliminated a key leader of the slavers, or perhaps they were too disorganized to mount an immediate response. Alternatively, they might have decided the cost of chasing us wasn't worth the potential losses, especially if they assessed their numbers as too depleted to engage effectively.

Regardless of the reason, we didn't let down our guard. We continued our trek, moving under the cover of night to avoid any potential late responses from Slab City. Our route took us around the north side of the Salton Sea, a strategic choice to put substantial natural barriers between us and any possible pursuers. This area provided us with not only physical cover but also strategic obscurity, as few would expect us to move towards the harsher terrains.

As we settled into a temporary camp far from Slab City, we kept our security tight. Each member of our group was vigilant, rotating watches throughout the night to ensure any approach by the slavers could be detected early. Despite the successful rescue, the tension of the escape left us all on high alert, prepared to move at a moment's notice if the situation changed.

Diverging Paths

After reaching a safe distance from Slab City, we finally allowed ourselves a moment to breathe and assess our situation. It was during this respite that one of the rescued captives shared alarming insights into the evolving dynamics within Slab City. According to their account, an emerging leader was exerting control over the disparate groups of slaves by force, quelling resistance through violent confrontations. This explained the lack of pursuit we experienced; the slavers were too preoccupied with internal power struggles to bother with a few escaped captives.

The information painted a grim picture: this new leader was gradually succeeding in unifying the slavers into a formidable organization. Moreover, they were reportedly seeking alliances with other hostile groups to the east, potentially amplifying their threat. The prospect of Slab City transforming into a consolidated force was a dire concern for Farm Bridge.

Given the urgent need for more intelligence, Ruslana decided on a swift return to Farm Bridge using boats to cross the Salton Sea. However, Watson and I chose a riskier route. We planned to head east, disguising ourselves as Raiders or scavengers looking to join the emerging coalition. Our goal was to infiltrate their ranks and gather critical information about their intentions and capabilities.

Ruslana was hesitant about our plan, fearing for our safety, but she ultimately respected our decision. As we prepared to part ways, she embraced me, expressing her gratitude and promising to fortify Farm Bridge against the potential threat. To Watson, she offered a heartfelt kiss on the cheek, acknowledging his bravery and the deep bond that had formed among us during our ordeals.

Watson blushed at the gesture, and there was a lingering moment of connection between them, hinting at deeper feelings that had developed. Despite the dangers ahead, this brief interlude of human warmth and solidarity bolstered our spirits as we set off on our separate paths, each group determined to protect what we cherished most.

Journey to Lake Havasu

Days 381-385 were spent navigating towards what we suspected might be the gathering point of the emerging horde—Lake

Havasu. The location was strategic, with its ample fresh water supply and major highways, making it a likely hub for a significant number of people. Watson and I traveled north from the Salton Sea, following State Route 111 to Interstate 10, which we planned to take east until reaching Highway 95 north towards Havasu.

Our journey was marked by the eerie silence of the highways, now just thoroughfares in a post-apocalyptic world. The rough calculations I made one evening revealed that over a year had passed since the collapse of civilization. The constant cool, cloudy weather, a result of global cooling caused by atmospheric dust, made the passage of time feel even more surreal.

Days 386 to 389 brought us to a critical point in our journey. As we approached the junction of Interstate 10 and another major route, we spotted a checkpoint from a distance. Reconnaissance was crucial, so we waited until nightfall to approach for a closer look. The checkpoint was manned by approximately fifteen Raiders, who had set up a rough barricade, controlling access along the highway.

This obstacle posed a significant risk; the Raiders were likely part of the larger force we were investigating, and their presence indicated we were close to our destination. The checkpoint's setup suggested they were well-organized, potentially under the command of the new leader uniting the disparate groups of Slab City and beyond. We needed to gather more information on their operations and find a way to bypass or overcome this checkpoint without drawing attention to ourselves.

Encounters at the Checkpoint

As Watson and I approached the heavily armed checkpoint where Interstate 10 met Highway 95, it was clear that these weren't just run-of-the-mill desert raiders; they were likely a significant fraction of the organized force we were investigating. Watson suggested a bold strategy: instead of avoiding them, we would introduce ourselves as potential recruits, leveraging his experience in handling such situations.

In broad daylight, we walked up to the outpost, our rifles non-threateningly slung over our shoulders. Watson took the lead in the conversation, addressing the group of raiders who greeted us with their guns drawn. He spun a tale of us being weary of scrounging from ruins and looking for a leader with a vision, someone planning big moves where we could contribute effectively.

The raiders initially responded with laughter, but their leader, a stern-looking individual, considered Watson's words more seriously. He confirmed that there was indeed an ambitious leader making significant plans, but he was not the one to decide on our recruitment. His role was limited to monitoring the highways and collecting 'taxes' from those who used these roads for trade.

I was taken aback to learn about the taxation system they had implemented. It seemed that even in this chaotic new world, some attempts at establishing order were emerging. The leader explained that while there was still plenty of raiding, especially against resistant communities, there were also structured allowances for these groups to conduct controlled 'hunting trips' outside their territories.

Curious about the identity of this commanding figure, we inquired further and were corrected on our assumption—it wasn't a 'he' but a 'her.' The leader was General Lecrae, a name that signaled her authority and perhaps her ambitions. This revelation added a new layer to our understanding of the power dynamics at play in the region, highlighting the complexity of the leadership that was consolidating power among the chaos.

Approaching Havasu

Days 390-394 brought us closer to Lake Havasu, revealing a disturbing yet organized scene. The road leading up to Havasu was surprisingly busy, hosting a mix of raiders, civilians, and even trading caravans. This scene bore the hallmarks of a harsh, emerging civilization under the rule of General Lecrae, known as The Iron Lady.

The civilians we observed bore a haunted look, the kind that comes from living under a strict and oppressive regime. The caravans were a mix of traders and slaves, reminiscent of ancient empires where order was maintained through fear and brutality. General Lecrae had established a system where looting, stealing, and fighting were strictly regulated, and every transaction or movement seemed to be taxed or controlled.

This burgeoning society was built on the principles of slavery, sanctioned violence, and absolute control. It was a civilization, albeit a cruel and unforgiving one, where The Iron Lady had successfully consolidated various survivor groups into a formidable force. She had not only unified these groups but had also imposed a vision of order that was both feared and respected.

Watson, who had spent much of his life as a loner in the mountains, found the constant stream of caravans and the visible hierarchy within Havasu unsettling. The stark contrast between his life of solitude and the strict governance of The Iron Lady's territory was palpable. As we entered Havasu, the true scale of this new society became apparent. Thousands of survivors had been drawn here, now living under the iron grip of a leader who had reshaped a collapsed world into her own image.

Days 395 to 399 found us navigating the complex social and military structures of Havasu Springs Resort, which now served as the southern base for The Iron Lady's operations. The city across the lake, Havasu City, was her main stronghold. Following Watson's lead, we approached a building designated for new recruits on the outskirts of the resort area. His demeanor, blending caution with a display of subtle strength, seemed to resonate well with the recruiters, who appreciated toughness and could smell fear or weakness a mile away.

Our initial interaction involved a bit of posturing from one of the would-be recruiters who tried to size us up with intimidation tactics. Watson's response, a careful mix of respect and veiled threat, earned us a nod of approval, and soon we were welcomed into the ranks of the Raider organization. However, due to the chaotic nature of their operations, we were informed that we would have to wait a few days before being fully integrated and assigned to a specific gang.

The organization was evidently attempting to meld various Raider groups and gangs into a unified force, a challenging task given the inherently selfish and anarchic nature of these groups. This effort was overseen by military veterans who brought a level of discipline and strategic planning to the otherwise unruly Raiders.

For the time being, we were placed in quarantine in makeshift barracks, allowed to leave but restricted in our movements within the community. This limitation made it challenging to gather the intelligence we desperately needed. As the days passed, my frustration grew. The restriction not only hindered our primary mission but also forced us to navigate the internal politics and power dynamics of this nascent military state, all while maintaining our cover and ensuring our safety in a volatile environment.

An Unexpected Reunion

Day 400 at the Havasu Springs Resort base was marked by a growing impatience and frustration. My mind was flooded with questions about The Iron Lady's identity, her plans, the scope of her command, and possible alliances against her. Each day spent without answers felt like a failure, as my friends' safety hung in the balance.

While navigating the confines of our limited freedom within the base, Watson continually reminded me of the importance of caution, sensing my restlessness. The base, once a bustling resort attracting tourists for its recreational amenities, was now a grim shadow of its former self. The tennis and basketball courts, once scenes of leisure and joy, were now frequented by raiders who had embraced a brutal survival strategy in this post-apocalyptic world.

As I walked away from the recreation area, disgusted by the sight and reminiscing about what the world had become, I accidentally bumped into a young woman carrying laundry. The collision sent her belongings scattering across the ground. My initial reaction was to help her, but the sight of a slave collar around her neck snapped me back to reality, and I grumbled a harsh rebuke to maintain my cover.

She hurried to gather her things, apologizing, her voice trailing off as our eyes met. The recognition was immediate. Christina, with her distinctive almond-shaped eyes and the familiar scar on her cheek from a childhood accident. My heart skipped a beat as the realization hit me—it was Christina, my ex-fiancée, who I hadn't seen since just before the catastrophe that ended the world.

Days 401 to 403 were consumed with shock and the complicated emotions of this reunion. Christina, visibly confused and cautious, asked if I was with "them" — referring to the raiders. The encounter left me reeling, forced to confront not only the past but also the immediate moral quandaries of our present circumstances.

CHAPTER 2:
TENSIONS AT HAVASU

Day 500 in Havasu Springs Resort brought a confrontation that shook me to the core. There, amidst the desolation of a raider camp, I faced Christina, my ex-fiancée, who was now a slave under the brutal control of raiders. The shock of seeing her in such a dire situation, combined with the unresolved emotions from our breakup, flooded me with confusion and anger. She had been the one to end our engagement, choosing her career over our relationship, and I had thought she moved to the East Coast. Yet, here she was, not far from where I had been all along.

The encounter was abruptly interrupted by a hulking man, clearly one of the slavers, who berated Christina for speaking with me. He claimed her as his property, wielding a menacing club modified with wood staples—a tool of oppression and pain, as evidenced by the bruises on Christina's back. The sight ignited a deep, visceral anger within me, urging me to violent action.

However, before I could act on impulse and reach for my hidden knife, Watson intervened. His quick reflexes stopped me from grabbing the weapon. Watson's timely grasp on my hand was not just a physical restraint but a stark reminder of our mission and the precariousness of our situation.

"Why would you jeopardize everything for a rash move?" Watson whispered urgently. His words struck a chord. In the midst of my emotional turmoil, I was forced to acknowledge the broader implications of my actions—not just for our undercover mission but for the safety of Christina and ourselves.

Christina, coerced by the slaver's threats, quickly resumed her chores, leaving me in a tumult of emotions. Watson's grip loosened, and he gave me a look that was both a warning and a reassurance. He understood my feelings but reminded me of the necessity of restraint.

"We need to think this through," Watson said, guiding me away from the scene and towards a quieter part of the camp. "There's a way to handle this, but not through brute force. Let's figure out our next move without drawing attention."

His advice was sound, yet my mind raced with conflicting thoughts. How could I protect Christina and maintain our cover? What could we possibly do to undermine The Iron Lady's regime from within? These questions, along with the shock of Christina's presence here, weighed heavily on me as we retreated to strategize our next steps.

Hidden Moments with Christina

Days 404-409 were spent navigating a delicate balance between our mission and my personal turmoil. I managed to learn Christina's routine well enough to steal brief, private moments with her. During these stolen times, she shared the harrowing details of her experience since the catastrophe. She had been in the valley when the bombs hit, and initially, she and a group of survivors had managed to fend for themselves. However, their luck ran out when they were captured by a band of raiders. The brutality she described was chilling—members of her group were not only killed but butchered for meat, and the survivors, including her, were sold into slavery.

Christina had first been put to work in one of the labor crews in the camp. Her current owner, a man named Saul, had bought her with intentions that went beyond mere labor. Initially, he wanted her as a wife, but her resistance had turned him cruel. He kept her alive only because killing her would not be profitable, relegating her to perform strenuous manual labor as punishment.

Hearing Christina's story fueled a rage in me that was hard to contain. The injustice of her situation and the pervasive nature of slavery in this camp disgusted me deeply. I confided in her about my role and the larger mission, explaining that any reckless action could jeopardize not only our safety but also the lives of many others at Big Bear and Farm Bridge.

Despite the emotional pain, I reassured Christina of my commitment to finding a way to help her without precipitating violence that could lead to greater suffering. We discussed potential strategies discreetly, focusing on gathering more information and looking for an opportune moment that could lead to her safe extraction.

The situation was a complex web of emotional conflicts and strategic decisions. As much as I despised what this camp stood for and what it had done to Christina, Watson's words echoed in my mind: the necessity of keeping our focus on the greater good, even amidst personal grief and anger. This tension between personal desire and mission objectives was a constant struggle as we plotted our next steps in this harsh, unforgiving environment.

Grappling with Moral Complexity

As days turned into weeks, my understanding of the raider

society deepened, revealing layers I hadn't anticipated. The compound, ruled under the harsh yet structured laws laid down by The Iron Lady, wasn't entirely what I expected from a society built by raiders. There were strict rules against stealing, public fighting, and unapproved killing within the territory. These laws were enforced with brutal efficiency—violence was not only a method of control but also a stark deterrent.

Our mentor, Robert, embodied the complexities of this world. A middle-aged man with a family, his rugged exterior belied a certain fairness and a survivalist's pragmatism that made him somewhat likable, despite his association with the raiders. He lived with his wife and child within the compound, and it was clear that he was committed to protecting his family in this ruthless environment.

The raider society's approach to governance was reminiscent of feudal times—a harsh regime where protection was offered in exchange for taxes. This protection racket was essentially extortion, but for many, it was a price worth paying for safety amidst chaos. The community was starkly divided into those who could enforce their will and those who had to comply to survive.

In this grim setting, I found it challenging to navigate my emotions and the mission's objectives. I was here to gather intelligence and potentially undermine The Iron Lady's regime, but daily interactions with individuals like Robert complicated the narrative of good versus evil. It was a reminder that societies, no matter how dystopian, are not monoliths; they are made up of individuals, each with their own stories and moral landscapes.

This realization didn't simplify my mission—it complicated it. As I plotted how to assist Christina and gather the needed intelligence, I had to constantly remind myself of the broader picture and the stakes involved. Every action had potential consequences, and in a society where violence was a quick solution, the risks were amplified. The dual challenge of maintaining my cover and maneuvering through this moral minefield tested me in ways I had never anticipated, sharpening my understanding of the thin line between survival and humanity in a post-apocalyptic world.

Mission with Robert and Reflections on Comradeship

Days 414 to 418 were spent on the road, fulfilling our first assignment with Robert: tax collecting from a farm that had ceased its agreed-upon shipments. This journey provided a prime opportunity to better understand my companions. Watson and I, despite our differing backgrounds, had formed a bond through our shared mission and the universal desire to protect our loved ones in this brutal new world. While Watson's rugged individualism and aloof demeanor often kept him at a distance, the circumstances had made him a trusted companion, if not a friend.

Robert, on the other hand, was surprisingly easy to get along with. Despite his role in the raider hierarchy, he exuded a warmth that was difficult to ignore. His pragmatic approach to survival and his evident care for his family humanized him, complicating my feelings towards the raiders. It was a reminder of the complexities of human nature: even those who serve harsh regimes can have commendable qualities.

As we traveled, I learned more about the "Army of the Sun," which Robert explained saw itself as a beacon of new civilization in the post-apocalyptic chaos. They believed they were restoring order to the wasteland, albeit through methods I found morally questionable. This mission to collect overdue taxes was part of maintaining that order, ensuring that agreements were honored and resources flowed within their controlled territories.

The farm we approached had been silent, not due to defiance but calamity. We discovered that a local disaster had struck, severely impacting their ability to produce. This revelation put Robert in a difficult position, balancing his duty to the Army of the Sun with his natural inclination towards fairness. Observing his decision-making process provided further insights into the raider's governance, which wasn't solely based on oppression but also on a rudimentary form of justice.

This blend of harshness and fairness, friendship and formality, was emblematic of the new societal norms taking root in this dystopian landscape. As we returned from the mission, my thoughts were with Christina, planning how to address her plight with Saul and wondering how the complexities of these human connections could be navigated to forge a path toward something better, even in such dark times.

Journey Through the Desert and Reflections

Days 419-422 saw us traveling deeper into the complexities of this reshaped world. As we ventured east past Lake Havasu, moving away from its relative civilization, the landscape reverted to the harsh, unforgiving desert. Lake Havasu City, now to our north, stood as a haunting reminder of what once was —a thriving community now just a ghost town swallowed by the desert and poisoned by the radiation that had spread in the aftermath of the nuclear catastrophe.

During our journey, the desolation around us mirrored the conversation topics that had grown increasingly somber. Robert's reflections on his choice to align with the Army of the Sun brought to light the desperate decisions faced by many in this new world. He spoke of the initial chaos that reigned after the fall, describing how The Iron Lady's rise to power had brought a semblance of order and safety. His acknowledgment of the moral compromises this entailed painted a picture of a man caught between survival and conscience.

Watson's interjection about the values worth dying for had struck a chord. It reminded us that even in times of dire necessity, the choices made could define the essence of one's character. His words seemed to weigh heavily on Robert, perhaps challenging his justifications or reinforcing his internal conflicts about the part he played in this regime.

This dialogue deepened my understanding of the raider society. It wasn't merely a group of opportunists exploiting the fallout of a collapsed civilization; it was also a community of individuals grappling with their choices, each with their own reasons and justifications. This realization added layers of gray to my previously black-and-white view of the raiders.

As we continued east, the stark, barren landscapes served as a constant reminder of the world's fragility and the thin line between civilization and chaos. The ghostly quiet of the abandoned towns we passed whispered stories of past lives and broken dreams, reinforcing the brutality of our current reality and the human struggle to find order in chaos.

A Confrontation in the Desert

As we neared the source of the gunshots, the tension among us was palpable. It was late in the evening, about a day's journey from our destination, when the sudden sound of gunfire cut through the quiet desert air. Robert's assurance echoed in my mind, reminding me of the stakes involved—not just for us, but for the entire community that might face severe retribution if they harmed any emissaries of the Army.

I pushed ahead of the group, driven by a mix of duty and adrenaline. Cresting a hill, I saw the aftermath of what looked like a brutal ambush. Several bodies lay scattered across the ground in a grim tableau of violence. Among the dead, a struggle was still unfolding—a man and an older woman fought desperately for survival.

The man, overpowering and aggressive, had the upper hand. He knocked the woman to her knees and attempted a brutal strike with the butt of his rifle. She dodged the first blow but wasn't quick enough to avoid the second, which landed heavily on her shoulder, eliciting a cry of pain.

Fueled by urgency, I sprinted toward the conflict, shouting to distract the attacker. My intervention gave the woman a momentary advantage, and she used it to knock her assailant off balance. However, he quickly regained his footing, pulled a pistol, and aimed it at her.

Realizing I was still too far to intervene directly, I stopped in my tracks. With years of training kicking in, I raised my M4 carbine, aimed through the sight, and waited for a clear shot. As soon as the man was in my sights, I pulled the trigger. The sound of the gunshot echoed across the open desert, momentarily overpowering the silence that followed. My action had halted what would have surely been a fatal outcome for the woman.

As the dust settled, the gravity of what had just occurred began to sink in. I approached the scene cautiously, aware that each step took me further into the complex moral landscape we navigated daily in this new world. This intervention, though necessary, would have repercussions, and as I helped the woman to her feet, I prepared myself for the challenges that lay ahead in dealing with the aftermath and continuing our mission.

Unexpected Ally in the Wasteland

Days 423-426 unfolded with an unexpected twist: the woman I saved from the ambush was none other than Evan, known widely as The Iron Lady, the formidable leader whose rule had reshaped the landscape of the region. This revelation shook me to the core. Here was the person responsible for the oppressive regime that I had been sent to undermine, yet in the chaos of the ambush, I had unwittingly become her savior.

As we made camp for the night, still reeling from the day's events, The Iron Lady, despite her injury and the recent attack, exuded a commanding presence that was unnervingly composed. Robert, who was as shocked as I was to discover her identity, greeted her with a mix of respect and disbelief. Her reputation preceded her, but meeting her in such circumstances painted a complex picture of a leader who was both feared and revered.

She introduced herself formally to me, acknowledging the life-saving shot with a nod of respect that belied her usual stern demeanor. Her strength and resilience were palpable, qualities that evidently drew people to her cause in these unstable times. Yet, it was her sharp intelligence and the strategic acumen reflected in her eyes that struck me the most—this was no ordinary leader but a tactician who had mastered the art of survival and control in a post-apocalyptic world.

Sitting around the campfire, The Iron Lady shared stories of her rise to power, how she had united fractious groups under her banner to bring order to the chaos. Her narrative was compelling, and I found myself understanding, if not entirely agreeing with, her methods. She spoke of her vision for a civilized society, one that could rise from the ashes of the old world, even if it meant making hard, often brutal decisions.

The situation was profoundly paradoxical. Here I was, tasked with gathering intelligence to potentially bring down her regime, yet now connected to her by a life-debt. This complex relationship underscored the murky moral waters of post-apocalyptic leadership and survival. As the night wore on, I pondered my next moves, aware that every decision from here on out carried weight beyond my initial mission. How would I navigate this newfound alliance while staying true to my ultimate goals? The days ahead promised to test my resolve and principles more than ever.

Philosophical Divergences

Days 427-430 in the company of The Iron Lady, Evan, led to deeper, more philosophical discussions. As Watson boldly questioned the morality of enslavement under her regime, I was tense, aware of the thin ice upon which he treated. Yet, Evan responded without a hint of offense. Her comparison of her rules to the ancient laws of the Old Testament was both unsettling and illuminating.

Evan explained that, much like the ancient laws that might seem harsh by modern standards, her rules were designed to provide structure and order in a world that had none. She argued that her laws were a necessary step forward from the anarchic chaos that prevailed after the apocalypse. According to her, these rules were not about oppression but about survival and rebuilding— a viewpoint that, while difficult to accept, offered a glimpse into her rationale.

She elaborated on her vision of civilization, stating that it was not the methods but the results that would define the success of her regime. The conversation shifted to the historical context of governance, where she cited examples of empires built on strict hierarchies and sometimes brutal control mechanisms that nonetheless resulted in prosperous societies.

Watson, ever the skeptic, pushed back against this reasoning, pointing out that the prosperity of such empires often came at the cost of countless lives and freedoms. His perspective sparked a spirited debate about the balance between order and freedom, a debate that resonated deeply with me as I struggled with my own internal conflicts about our mission and my burgeoning respect for Evan's leadership capabilities.

This dialogue made it clear that Evan was no ordinary leader; she was a thinker, a planner, and a survivor who believed deeply in her mission. Her ability to articulate a vision of order in the post-apocalyptic chaos was compelling, yet the moral implications of her methods remained a significant concern.

As the night deepened, so did my contemplation on the complexities of leadership and morality in a world reborn from ashes. The conversation with Evan, marked by its depth and intensity, highlighted the philosophical divide between our ideals and the harsh realities of the new world order she was trying to establish. This encounter underscored the challenging decisions that lay ahead, not just for me, but for all who lived under her rule and those of us poised to challenge it.

Journey with The Iron Lady

Days 427-429 brought new dimensions to our journey as The Iron Lady, Evan, decided it would be safer for her and her two remaining men to travel with our group back to Havasu. This decision presented an opportunity not just for security, but for deeper insights into the character of this enigmatic leader.

As we traversed the harsh desert terrain, I found a moment to speak with Evan privately, away from the ears of the rest of our party. This rare chance to converse without the immediate influence of her followers allowed for a more candid dialogue about her visions and the justifications for her controversial methods.

During our walk, Evan shared more about her strategic approach to leadership in the post-apocalypse. She emphasized the concept of interim rules—a necessary governance to shepherd her people through the instability post-collapse, much like the ancient laws she referenced. Her comparison was not lost on me; it highlighted her pragmatism in using historical models to legitimize her harsh rule.

Evan was open about the challenges she faced. "Leadership in such times isn't about making popular decisions but necessary ones," she explained. "It's about setting a course that can eventually lead to stability, even if it means making tough choices now."

I pressed her about the sustainability of such a model and whether she truly believed her society could evolve beyond its current authoritarian state. She was thoughtful, acknowledging that while her current system was far from ideal, it was a calculated step towards re-establishing order and, eventually, a more balanced society.

"Our goal isn't to remain in this state forever," Evan confided. "But to stabilize, grow, and evolve. Just as societies of old outgrew their primitive laws, we too aim to develop laws that are more just and humane, once we're capable of upholding them."

As we continued our journey back to Havasu, I reflected on her words. The realization that her followers not only respected but idolized her added a complex layer to my understanding of her leadership. They saw her not just as a ruler but as a visionary capable of guiding them through the apocalypse to a hopeful resurgence. This devotion made my mission all the more complicated, intertwining respect, fear, and the undeniable effectiveness of her governance in creating a cohesive society out of chaos.

A Meeting at the Ranch

Days 430 to 435 brought us to the doorstep of the ranch responsible for the unpaid taxes, a homestead now running on the brink of medieval subsistence. The family, consisting of a husband, wife, and their four children, ages ranging from 16 to 23, greeted us with a mix of awe and fear—particularly upon recognizing The Iron Lady. In another life, the older children might have been in college, but now, their future was tethered to the arid soil and the health of their livestock.

Evan, The Iron Lady, approached the matter with unexpected calmness. Her presence alone commanded attention, yet she employed no threats or harsh words as she began her inquiry about the missing taxes. Her demeanor was stern yet fair, and it was clear she understood the dire straits many of these outlying families found themselves in.

The family patriarch, visibly nervous, explained the situation. Their main water pump had broken down, and without it, their crop yields had plummeted, severely affecting their ability to meet the tax demands. It was a stark reminder of how fragile life had become, where something as simple as a broken pump could jeopardize not only the livelihood but the survival of an entire family.

Evan listened intently, her face a mask of contemplation. After a moment of silence, she spoke, not with the voice of a tyrant, but with the pragmatism of a leader faced with the realities of her territory. She proposed a solution that took me by surprise— a compromise that involved the family committing to a reduced tax payment plan until they could repair their pump and get back on their feet. In return, she would provide the necessary mechanical parts and send one of her engineers to assist in the repair.

This act of leniency was a tactical move that served multiple purposes: it maintained her image as a fair leader, ensured future compliance, and stabilized her resource inflow from the ranch. As she outlined her plan, I could see the relief mixed with gratitude in the family's eyes, and I realized that Evan's governance, while harsh, was not devoid of mercy or practical wisdom.

The resolution of this tax issue underlined the complex nature of Evan's rule—it was an iron fist in a velvet glove, combining strength with a keen sense of sustainability. As we left the ranch, I reflected on the delicate balance of power and empathy, authoritarianism and pragmatism, that defined her leadership. This encounter deepened my understanding of her methods and her ability to command loyalty, even from those who feared her.

Stark Realities and Moral Dilemmas

In the tense atmosphere of the rancher's homestead, The Iron Lady's interrogation deepened. As the family explained the loss of their cattle due to tainted water, Evan detailed the purpose of the taxes with a calm that belied the underlying sternness of her message. Her explanation of tax usage was strategic, designed to remind the ranchers of their obligations not just to her authority, but to the stability of the entire region.

"Your taxes," she explained, "fund the efforts to repair critical infrastructure and maintain the security that shields this community from the chaos that predates my command." Her tone was instructive yet carried a sharp edge that surfaced as she outlined the consequences of non-compliance. "When you withhold resources, it not only affects my ability to sustain and arm the troops but also endangers every other family who counts on us for protection."

The gravity of her words weighed heavily in the air, casting a shadow of fear across the rancher's face. The implication was clear: their failure to contribute risked more than their own welfare; it threatened the collective security that had been hard-fought under her rule.

The atmosphere grew heavier as Evan turned her attention to the broader implications of their actions, suggesting that selfishness in times of scarcity amounted to an indirect theft from the community. "What is the penalty for theft?" she asked rhetorically, her gaze sweeping over the anxious faces of the family.

At this moment, I felt the acute moral ambiguity of our mission. The fear in the rancher's eyes and the tension among his family made me question where my loyalties truly lay. As a soldier under Evan's command, my duty was clear, but as a person who had seen the cost of such harsh governance, my conscience was troubled.

I caught the eye of the oldest son, who looked like he might be holding back a defiant or desperate reaction. My hand twitches involuntarily toward my weapon, a reflex born of too many unpredictable moments in this harsh landscape. What would happen if this situation escalated? Which side would I choose?

This moment underscored the complex interplay of power, responsibility, and survival in the new world Evan was striving to build. It highlighted not only the harsh necessities of post-apocalyptic governance but also the personal conflicts that arose when enforcing such stringent laws. As we left the ranch, I remained introspective, wrestling with the difficult choices that lay ahead and the role I would play in shaping this unforgiving new world.

Return to Havasu

Days 436 to 440 were consumed by a palpable tension as we made our way back to Havasu. The incident at the ranch had left deep scars, not only on the family we had visited but within our own group. Watson's auctions, while saving me from having to commit a horrendous act, had introduced a rift between us. He had taken the burden of the execution upon himself, perhaps to protect me or simply because he had already adapted to the harsh realities of The Iron Lady's regime.

As we traveled back, Watson kept to himself, his demeanor closed off. The silence between us was heavy, filled with unasked questions and unvoiced judgments. I could feel the weight of his judgment and perhaps his resentment for my hesitation at the ranch.

Robert, ever the mediator, tried to engage me, likely intending to offer some form of consolation or to help rationalize what had happened. However, I was not in a place to hear it. My mind was a tumult of emotions—guilt, anger, confusion. I dismissed him, not out of disrespect, but from a desperate need to sort through my thoughts without the intrusion of well-meaning platitudes.

The Iron Lady had watched the entire scene unfold with a calculating eye, evaluating my reaction, Watson's decisiveness, and the overall loyalty of her troops. Her leadership style, while effective in maintaining order, thrived on instilling fear and obedience, qualities she valued over any moral objections her laws might raise.

As we neared Havasu, the reality of what our return might mean began to sink in. A reckoning was inevitable. Watson's auctions, while perhaps saving us both in the short term, had opened up a chasm that would need to be addressed. How we would reconcile this, or if it was even possible, remained uncertain. The barracks, once a place of respite, now felt like a looming battleground where ideologies and personal loyalties would clash.

In the days leading up to our return, I grappled with the stark choices laid before me. Aligning fully with The Iron Lady's methods was untenable, yet defiance seemed equally fraught with danger. The line between survival and complicity had blurred, and finding a path that maintained one's moral integrity while ensuring physical safety had become the challenge of every day in this new world order.

Wound Care in the Wilderness

After my fall down the rocky hillside, the pain and the deep cut on my arm became my immediate focus, overshadowing the emotional turmoil of the day's earlier events. That evening, as we made camp, The Iron Lady, Evan, took it upon herself to inspect and treat my injury. Her actions were precise and indicated a familiarity with field medicine that commanded respect.

Under the dim light of the campfire, she removed the makeshift bandage I had applied, her expression turning serious as she assessed the wound. "This is bad, really bad," she commented before quickly fetching a first aid kit equipped with the essentials for more thorough treatment.

With a bottle of alcohol and a short knife, she prepared to clean the wound more aggressively. "Hang on," she warned, signaling the pain that was to come. She expertly sliced open part of the wound to ensure no dirt or debris remained embedded within. The sharp sting of alcohol poured into the open cut made me clench my teeth, but I understood the necessity of her actions.

"You've got decent first aid skills," Evan observed, "but this cut is too deep for a simple bandage." She explained the risk of infection due to the debris pushed into the wound by the fall. "When that rock pierced the skin, it shoved all the dirt and whatever else was on your skin deep into the flesh. Flushing it with alcohol helps get all the foreign debris out."

After thoroughly cleaning the wound, Evan proceeded to sew it shut with practiced skill, ensuring each stitch was placed to promote healing and minimize scarring. "You probably already got some germs in you," she noted, handing me a bottle of antibiotics. "Take these twice a day. Make sure you finish the course to prevent any infection from taking hold."

As she worked, I felt a grudging respect for her competence and her no-nonsense approach to crisis management. Her hands were steady, her focus unyielding, and in that moment, she was not just a leader of a controversial regime but a caretaker ensuring the well-being of someone under her command.

This encounter added yet another layer to my understanding

of Evan. Her ability to toggle between the roles of leader, medic, and mentor showcased her complexity and reinforced the multifaceted nature of survival in this new world. As she finished bandaging the wound, I was left to contemplate the duality of her character—a ruler who could be both ruthless in her governance and yet undeniably capable of empathy and care.

A Vision of Expansion

Days 441-445 brought us through a detour en route to Havasu, as Evan directed us to visit one of the smaller encampments set up by the Army of the Dawn. This outpost served multiple functions: it was a crucial hub for patrols maintaining order within the territory and a vital link in the supply chain connecting the various military posts that enforced the boundaries of Evan's burgeoning state.

As we approached the encampment, the scale of Evan's ambitions became increasingly evident. The outpost, while modest, was buzzing with activity. Soldiers coordinated patrols and logistics with a professionalism that belied the rough conditions of their environment. Supplies were being distributed, strategies discussed, and reports on regional security shared. This was not merely a military camp; it was a nerve center for the expansion and consolidation of power within the newly claimed territories.

Evan took the opportunity to explain her vision for the future. "In time, these roads will be rebuilt, and the perimeter posts will transform into permanent fortifications," she outlined. Her tone was filled with a mix of resolve and pride as she gestured towards the horizon where, one day, new roads would connect a network of fortified towns and cities.

"This land was once lawless, a place where survival was the

only law. We're changing that. We're building something lasting here," she continued, her eyes scanning the bustling activity around us. "Yes, the methods are tough, and the decisions are harder still. But without them, there would be no progress, only perpetual chaos."

As I observed the efficiency and order of the encampment, I had to admit the stark contrast with the smaller, more isolated communities like Farm Bridge and Big Bear. While they managed to maintain a semblance of peace, they lacked the resources and coordination that Evan's military organization provided. Her approach, though undeniably harsh, brought a level of stability and security that was hard to dismiss.

The visit to the encampment left me with a profound sense of the complexities involved in nation-building in this post-apocalyptic world. Evan was not merely surviving; she was orchestrating the birth of a new civilization from the ashes of the old, using both fear and structure as her tools. Whether this vision justified the means—particularly the violence and control—remained a difficult question. Yet, it was clear that her leadership was forging a path towards a future that, while forged in the crucible of harsh realities, held the promise of stability and order for thousands.

The Massacre at the Encampment

Days 436 to 451 were marked by a grim discovery that underscored the volatile and perilous nature of the wasteland. As we approached the encampment, the absence of a greeting party was our first ominous sign, contrary to the strict protocol that should have ensured a 24-hour guard. The setup was familiar to anyone with military experience—sand-filled Hesco barriers similar to those used in conflict zones like Iraq and Afghanistan, complemented by partially constructed guard towers. Yet, it was eerily silent.

The smell hit us first, a pungent stench that no training could prepare you for. But nothing could have prepared us for the sight within the perimeter: a massacre. The bodies of soldiers were strewn about, a grotesque tableau of death that spoke of intense violence. It was clear that this was not just an attack; it was a statement. Each body had been desecrated, stripped of clothing, with symbols carved into their flesh, some still bound by ropes indicating the horror they faced while alive.

The Iron Lady, Evan, drew close to whisper, her voice a mix of rage and solemnity. "You wonder why my methods can be so harsh? This is why. Take it all in." Her directive was chilling, as it forced me to confront the harsh realities that justified her ruthless governance. This scene was a stark illustration of the threats that lurked outside the order she was trying to establish.

No survivors were visible, nor were there any bodies of the attackers, only the dead and the ominous silence of a ghostly battlefield. The missing families suggested either abduction or forced recruitment, a common terror tactic to break the spirits of any who opposed.

Who—or what—could execute such a ferocious attack? The encampment had been designed to withstand assaults from raiders and bandits, suggesting that the attackers were extraordinarily powerful, or perhaps that there was an insidious betrayal from within.

This massacre was not just a physical assault; it was a psychological one, intended to instill fear and demonstrate that no one, not even an army as formidable as the Army of the Dawn, was immune to the chaos of the wasteland. As we left the site, the weight of this realization sat heavy on my shoulders, complicating my feelings about The Iron Lady's harsh tactics. Were they truly a necessary evil in a world so brutally lawless, or was there another way to bring order without descending into the cycle of violence and retribution she so often employed?

These questions haunted me as we made our way back to Havasu, each step away from the carnage a step deeper into the moral quagmire that this new world presented.

A New Threat Emerges

As we dealt with the aftermath of the massacre, Evan directed us to construct a large bonfire to honor her fallen soldiers, refusing to leave them for scavengers. She joined in the grueling task, displaying a somber reverence as we arranged the bodies. Despite her harsh reputation and the manipulative tactics she employed to maintain control, her genuine care for her troops was evident, adding yet another layer to her complex persona.

During this grim work, Evan shared information about the attackers, a group known as the AzTechos. This group was composed largely of survivors who had traveled north from Mexico, many of whom were former cartel members. They had adopted and adapted ancient practices, claiming to draw from Aztec traditions, including the use of powerful hallucinogens and what they called "blood magic." This pseudo-religious, militant group lived in a state of constant warfare, often raiding communities, taking slaves, and performing ritual sacrifices.

The AzTechos had grown into a formidable force, challenging even the might of Evan's Army of the Dawn. Their lack of organization, due to their erratic and psychopathic behavior, was the only thing that had prevented them from overrunning more territories. However, the recent attack had marked a significant and alarming escalation. It was deeply concerning that they had managed to penetrate so deeply into Evan's territory, bypassing border defenses to strike at one of the more secure inland posts.

This strategic and brutal raid underscored a critical vulnerability in the defenses of the Army of the Dawn and highlighted the growing threat posed by the AzTechos. Evan was visibly troubled by this development, aware that if the AzTechos could organize under a single, cohesive leadership, they could potentially overpower her structured military regime.

As we watched the flames consume the pyre, the weight of this new threat settled over us. The challenge was not only the immediate danger posed by the AzTechos but also the potential for further incursions if they continued to evolve from disorganized bands into a unified force. This threat necessitated a reassessment of defensive strategies and possibly a shift in how Evan's army would need to operate to counter this new, unpredictable enemy.

The realization that we were up against an enemy that embraced chaos as a weapon was chilling. As the night drew on, the crackling of the fire seemed to echo the unrest brewing on the horizon, a stark reminder of the continuous struggle for survival and dominance in this harsh, new world.

Reunion and Resolve

Days 452-457 brought a mixture of relief and renewed determination. After the harrowing events at the encampment and the recognition of my actions in saving Evan's life, she expedited my official integration into the Army of the Dawn, along with Watson. We were granted our own accommodations within the Havasu stronghold—a mark of our elevated status in her eyes.

Evan's cryptic mention of handling "personal business" was clearly a nod towards resolving the situation with Christina, a task she had left to my discretion as long as it remained discreet. Once back in Havasu, I wasted no time. The newfound freedom to move about the stronghold allowed me to seek out Christina without the usual restrictions.

As I navigated through the stronghold, I could feel the weight of many eyes on me. News of my deed had spread, and with it came a mix of respect and envy from others within the ranks. To some, Evan was more than a leader; she was a savior of sorts, and anyone closely associated with her garnered a mixture of awe and suspicion.

I found Christina in one of the workshops, ostensibly collecting supplies for Saul, her owner. The term still churned my stomach, but my focus was entirely on her well-being. As she turned and our eyes met, there was a fleeting smile on her face, quickly suppressed, yet unmistakable. It was a small, radiant moment in the grim shadows of our reality. However, the sight of new bruises marring her face ignited a fierce protectiveness in me.

"Christina," I started, my voice barely above a whisper, mindful of our surroundings. "I'm going to get you out of here. I have a plan."

Her initial reaction was a mix of hope and fear, a silent question in her eyes about the feasibility of such a promise. I explained that Evan had given me a certain leverage and freedom within the stronghold, which I intended to use to her advantage. We discussed potential strategies discreetly, weighing the risks and timing of each option.

The plan was dangerous and required precise execution. It

would involve creating a plausible scenario in which Saul could be discreetly incapacitated or eliminated without drawing direct suspicion to either of us. The logistics were daunting, but the determination to free Christina from her bondage—and from the man who had hurt her—strengthened my resolve.

As we parted ways that day, with a plan beginning to take shape, the path forward was fraught with peril. Yet, the promise of her freedom, and perhaps a chance for us to start anew, offered a beacon of hope. The next steps would be critical, demanding caution, cunning, and courage in equal measure.

The Plan in Motion

Days 458 to 466 were spent in careful preparation and observation. Using the resources at my disposal—extra rations and a newfound position of influence—I enlisted the help of local street urchins to gather intelligence on Saul. These children, savvy and adept at navigating the stronghold unnoticed, became my eyes and ears, tracking Saul's every move.

Saul's routine was predictable, revolving around his daily management of his properties and the poor treatment of his slaves. His home, a commandeered two-story townhouse, reflected his brutish lifestyle. He didn't bother locking his slaves in their room; the psychological chains of fear and domination were strong enough to keep them from even thinking about escape.

As the days passed, the pieces of my plan slowly fell into place. I noted the times Saul was most vulnerable, particularly when he was alone in his office late at night, absorbed in whatever cruelties or plans he concocted. The layout of his house, his habits, the comings and goings of his few trusted associates—all were cataloged meticulously.

The final plan was simple yet risky. It involved sneaking into his home under the cover of darkness, using a quiet back entrance that the urchins had discovered. The children had noticed that Saul often left his window slightly ajar to let out cigar smoke, a habit that now provided a silent entry point.

I decided against telling Christina any details of the plan. The less she knew, the safer she would be, regardless of the outcome. My aim was to confront Saul directly, to incapacitate him without alerting his guards or the slaves, thereby minimizing the risk of a violent altercation. If necessary, I was prepared to use lethal force, but I hoped it wouldn't come to that.

Days 463 to 466 were spent finalizing every detail, checking and double-checking each step. I equipped myself with the necessary tools—a quiet, non-lethal takedown was preferred. The plan was set for late night on the 466th day, just after Saul's usual late evening drink when he would be most vulnerable.

As the night approached, my resolve hardened. This was not just about freeing Christina; it was about taking a stand against the brutality that had permeated this new world under The Iron Lady's rule. It was a chance to prove that justice could be served without descending into the lawlessness that she so often preached against. As I readied myself, the weight of what was about to happen settled in. Success meant freedom for Christina and a significant blow to the corrupt power structure. Failure was not an option.

Confrontation in the Dark

As the moon hung low in the sky, casting long shadows across the desolate landscape, I found myself perched on the edge of Saul's roof, cloaked in darkness. The window was indeed open, just as I had hoped, a slight breeze whispering through the gap that invited me into the lion's den. With no air conditioning and the residual heat of a nuclear-cooled desert night seeping through the walls, it was the only relief from the stifling heat Saul could afford.

Silently, I slipped through the window, my body tensed for action, every sense sharpened. The room was dimly lit by the ambient light of the moon, casting a pale glow across Saul's sleeping form. He was turned away from me, his breathing deep and even, oblivious to the impending danger.

In my hand, I held a knife—its blade cold and precise, a stark contrast to the hot, pulsing blood it was about to spill. My training had prepared me for moments like this, yet nothing could fully prepare a man for the weight of taking another life, even one as despicable as Saul's. The plan was to strike swiftly at the base of his spine, a blow that would paralyze him instantly and silently. It was a clinical, calculated move meant to incapacitate without a struggle.

However, as I stood over him, knife poised, a moment of hesitation washed over me. The gravity of the act, the finality of it, weighed heavily on my conscience. Was there truly no other way? Could justice only be served through such violent means? The memory of Alexis, her ideals and her spirit, flickered in my mind, reinforcing my turmoil.

It was then, in that fleeting second of doubt, that Saul rolled over. His eyes, wide with shock and fear, met mine. The element of surprise was lost, and the room was suddenly charged with a new, dangerous energy. Saul's hand darted under his pillow, likely reaching for a weapon.

Instinct took over. I lunged forward, not with the intention to kill, but to neutralize the threat he posed. The knife drove down, not towards his spine, but his arm, pinning it to the bed and preventing him from drawing his weapon. Saul let out a muffled cry of pain, his body writhing under the sudden assault.

"Don't move," I hissed, pressing the blade slightly deeper to emphasize the seriousness of my threat. My heart raced, adrenaline flooding my system as I assessed the situation. I needed to control it quickly before it escalated any further. My plan had been to silence Saul permanently, but now, faced with the reality of his vulnerability and my own, I wondered if incapacitation might suffice to free Christina without further bloodshed.

This moment of hesitation could cost me, yet it also opened up a new path—one that might allow me to maintain my humanity in this harsh, unforgiving world.

Gasping for air and fighting for my life, I managed to free my arm from under Saul's crushing weight. His body was still heavy on mine, and every second under him felt like an eternity. As I struggled, I caught a glimpse of Christina standing in the doorway, a heavy wrench clutched in her trembling hands. It was she who had delivered the decisive blows that had saved me from being choked to death.

With a surge of adrenaline, I shoved Saul's limp body off me and scrambled to my feet, panting heavily from the exertion and the near-death experience. Christina dropped the wrench, her face pale and shocked, her eyes wide with the horror of what she had just done.

"Saul?" she stammered, her voice barely above a whisper, her gaze fixed on his still form.

I moved quickly to check his pulse. He was alive but unconscious, the side of his head swollen and bloody from Christina's desperate intervention. I knew we didn't have much time; we needed to act fast before he regained consciousness or someone came to investigate the noise.

"Christina, we need to leave. Now," I urged, my voice firm despite my ragged breaths. The urgency of the situation seemed to snap her out of her shock, and she nodded, her expression set with a newfound resolve.

I quickly gathered a few essentials from the room—some cash, keys, and whatever small valuables I could stuff into my pockets. Christina did the same, moving mechanically, driven by the adrenaline and the fear of the consequences if we were caught.

With one last look at Saul, ensuring he was still breathing but incapacitated, we slipped out of the townhouse into the cool night air. The streets were deserted at this late hour, which worked in our favor. We moved quickly and quietly, avoiding the main roads and taking the back alleys instead.

Our destination was the outskirts of Havasu, where I had previously arranged for a contact to meet us with a vehicle. Every shadow made us jump, every distant sound had us pausing, hearts pounding as we anticipated pursuit. But fortune seemed to favor us in those tense moments, and we reached the meeting point without incident.

The contact, a trusted fellow member of the Army of the Dawn who was disillusioned like me, was waiting with an old but reliable truck. We didn't waste time with pleasantries. Christina climbed into the back, hidden under a tarp, while I took the passenger seat. As the truck started with a rumble, I allowed myself a brief moment of relief. We were leaving Havasu behind, and with it, a life of servitude and brutality. The road ahead would be fraught with its own dangers, but for the first time in a long while, there was a glimmer of hope for a new beginning.

A Haunted Freedom

Days 467-470 were a mix of relief and silent turmoil. Christina and her two friends, now free from Saul's clutches, settled into the safety of the accommodation I shared with Watson. A discreet communication to The Iron Lady ensured that the incident with Saul was neatly swept under the rug. His disappearance raised no eyebrows, and the reclamation of his slaves was accepted without question among the ranks. At night, I held Christina close, trying to offer her comfort, but the space between us was more than physical. She was haunted, withdrawn into herself, grappling with the violence that had led to her freedom.

On the second night, as I tried to bridge the gap with a kiss, Christina recoiled. The pain in her voice was palpable as she confessed, "I can't stop seeing Saul's body. I know he did terrible things, but I killed him. Now every time I look at you, I just think about what I did." The weight of her first kill hung heavily between us. It was a barrier forged by the grim necessity of her actions, a stark reminder that the scars of violence are not only physical but also deeply emotional.

I didn't press her; I understood too well. Despite the brutality she had endured over the past year, taking a life had crossed a personal threshold for her, one that changed how she saw herself—and how she saw me. My role in her violent liberation had inadvertently distanced her further from me, a consequence I hadn't fully anticipated.

Days 471-474 brought more changes. The Iron Lady, ever strategic, had fortified her headquarters at the old government building in Lake Havasu City. Security was tight, with all but one entrance sealed off to funnel potential threats through a heavily guarded main entry. This fortress-like approach was a testament to the enemies she had made, and the lengths she would go to maintain her power.

As I navigated this fortified compound, I couldn't help but reflect on the parallels between Evan's stronghold and the emotional fortresses we build around ourselves. Just as The Iron Lady shielded herself from physical threats, Christina was building walls to protect her psyche from the trauma she had endured. Both were fortifications against the world, one made of concrete and steel, the other of psychological barriers.

In those days, as I moved through the heavily secured corridors of power, I pondered the complexities of freedom and the cost of security. Freedom had been won for Christina, but at what price to her soul? And as The Iron Lady continued to tighten her grip on power, I wondered about the ultimate cost of such security to all of us living under her rule. The answers were as elusive as the shadows that played across the walls of the Lake Havasu stronghold.

Strategic Insights and Tensions

Days 471-474 saw Watson and I entering The Iron Lady's fortified headquarters. The atmosphere was tense between us, neither having discussed the unsettling events at the ranch. Despite this, our mission required utmost professionalism and focus. As intelligence officers, our role was to absorb every piece of information, every nuance of conversation that could be strategically valuable.

The war room, once a conference room, now served as the strategic heart of The Iron Lady's operations. A massive map dominated the space, detailed with push pins in various colors marking the expanse of her territory and beyond. The red pins sketched the boundaries of her domain, stretching significantly more towards the East than the West, indicating minimal expansion towards California. This was a relief in some ways, suggesting a lesser immediate threat to the regions from which we had come.

Green pins within the territory marked critical locations such as forts and outposts. My eyes traced the line to the outpost recently devastated by the Aztecos, noting its strategic placement. It was clear that these positions were vital for maintaining control and security within her borders.

To the East and South, where the threat from the Aztecos was more pronounced, black pins peppered the map. These marked known strongholds of the Aztecos, with a disturbing number clustering close to the borders of The Iron Lady's territory. This visual representation of the threat laid out so starkly on the map brought home the scale of the challenge we faced. The concentration of enemy strongholds along these borders painted a grim picture of potential conflicts and the ongoing struggle for power in this post-apocalyptic landscape.

As Watson and I absorbed the strategic layout, the distance between us felt more profound. His earlier actions, while perhaps necessary from his perspective, had created a rift that was hard to bridge. Here in this war room, surrounded by markers of conflict and power, the personal and professional collided, making it difficult to separate feelings from duty.

Yet, as we stood side by side, reviewing intelligence

and planning our next moves, there was an unspoken understanding that, despite personal grievances, our collaboration was crucial. Not just for the success of our mission, but for the potential impact our actions could have on the broader struggle for stability and peace in this ravaged world.

As the briefing concluded, The Iron Lady turned to address the room. Her demeanor was composed, her voice firm, as she outlined the next steps in reinforcing the outposts and preparing for possible incursions. Her strategic acumen was evident, as was her ability to command respect and instill loyalty. However, beneath the surface, the complexities of leadership, loyalty, and morality in such turbulent times continued to challenge us all.

Mobilization and Uncertainty

Days 478 to 480 marked the onset of an all-out preparation for war. The usual silence of the post-apocalyptic landscape was shattered by the roar of engines. Four Stryker armored vehicles, a relic from the old military era, now repurposed for the needs of The Iron Lady's forces, lined up in the staging area outside of Lake Havasu City's fortified command center.

The area buzzed with activity as men and women, soldiers of the Army of the Dawn, loaded supplies into trailers attached to the Strykers. These vehicles, equipped to transport a company's worth of equipment, were vital for the upcoming operation. Their heavy-duty frames and firepower were necessary for the first wave of the assault, providing cover and establishing a foothold in the targeted area.

As the Strykers rumbled to life, I felt a mix of adrenaline and apprehension. The rest of us were to follow on foot, a grueling task given the desert terrain and the distance to cover. The objective was clear: to join forces with those already positioned at Greenwood by the Big Sandy River. These troops had moved ahead earlier, tasked with setting up a preliminary base from which we could launch coordinated strikes.

The Iron Lady's strategy was aggressive yet calculated. With enemy forces inching closer to our territories, particularly around the strategic points near Phoenix and Mexicali, there was no room for delay. The pin on Mexicali, disturbingly close to Farm Bridge, indicated a potential threat that could not be ignored. The removed pin near Big Bear suggested a reevaluation of threats or perhaps a previous skirmish that had altered strategic priorities.

As we readied ourselves, checking gear and securing body armor, The Iron Lady reviewed the plans with her commanders. Her presence was formidable, her command unequivocal. "This isn't just about defense," she stated firmly. "It's about making a statement that any threat to our territory is a threat to our survival."

Watson and I exchanged a wary glance. The memories of the incident at the ranch still lingered between us, an unspoken tension that we both knew would need to be addressed. However, the immediate demand of the situation left little room for personal grievances. We were soldiers in her army now, and the coming days would test not just our loyalty to her command but our own limits of endurance and moral fortitude.

As the Strykers led the way, dust kicking up under their heavy treads, I strapped on my helmet and adjusted my rifle. The sounds of war were a harsh reminder of the world we now inhabited—a world where peace was a fragile, fleeting concept, and survival depended on strength, strategy, and sometimes, sheer will. The march to Greenwood would be long and fraught with danger, but it was a path we had to walk, a duty we were bound to fulfill.

Departure and Reflection

As I prepared to leave with the Army of the Dawn, the weight of my actions and the complexities of my relationships weighed heavily on my mind. Christina's tearful eyes and tight embrace conveyed a mixture of fear and unresolved emotions. Her presence, once a source of comfort, now reminded me of the deep scars our experiences had inflicted on us both. I reassured her that I would return, trying to believe in my own words as much as I wanted her to believe them.

Standing by the rumbling armored vehicles, ready to depart, I reflected on the massive capabilities of The Iron Lady's forces. Equipped with a fleet of armored combat vehicles and an ample supply of stabilized fuel—a rarity in this fractured world—her army was a formidable power. The engineers and chemists among her ranks had ensured that, unlike most remnants of civilization, her military machine could operate at full capacity. This logistical advantage made her nearly invincible in a land where such resources were scarce.

As I looked back at Christina, I realized how much had changed between us. The hardships we had endured together and the violent circumstances I had exposed her to had altered our relationship irreversibly. She had once left me in the old world, and now, despite all my efforts to save her, she seemed distant, perhaps still resenting the role I had forced upon her. It mirrored the fear I had always had with Alexis—of being ultimately incompatible, of love marred by the harsh realities of life.

At that moment, as the engine of the nearest vehicle roared to life, signaling the time to move out, a part of me wondered if I indeed belonged with this army. Despite the doubts and the moral quandaries it presented, it felt like a place where my skills and experiences could be of use, where the clarity of military objectives overshadowed the complexities of personal relationships.

Saying goodbye to Christina did not hurt as much as I had expected. This realization was both liberating and saddening. It underscored the transformation I had undergone since rejoining the fight for survival in this post-apocalyptic world. As the convoy started to move, I took one last look at her, committing her image to memory, uncertain of what the future held but ready to face it head-on.

With each mile we traveled away from Havasu, I felt the distance growing not just in miles but in the emotional gulf between my past life and my present. The journey ahead was fraught with danger and uncertainty, but it was a path I had chosen, one that I would walk with the determination and resolve that had been forged in the fires of the world's end.

On the March to Greenwood

Days 481-486 saw Watson and I marching alongside the troops of the Army of the Dawn, though not formally assigned to any particular unit. Evan's strategy seemed to hinge on leveraging our skills for reconnaissance behind enemy lines —a task we were unwittingly well-prepared for, given our own secret intentions. Despite the complex feelings I harbored about fighting alongside an army that potentially threatened everything I held dear back home, there was a camaraderie that could not be ignored.

As we advanced towards Greenwood, positioned on the eastern

edge of The Iron Lady's territory, our roles within the army afforded us a certain level of respect and, unavoidably, the envy of other soldiers. This informal status allowed us a degree of flexibility in our movements and actions, which could prove essential for our covert reconnaissance mission.

Robert, who marched with us, had become more than just a fellow soldier over these days. His decency and the tough decisions he had been forced to make in this harsh new world painted a picture of a man doing his best under dire circumstances. It was a reminder that within the ranks, there were many who, like Robert, were not inherently cruel or evil but simply trying to survive.

Our company, consisting of about 120 soldiers, moved with purpose towards Greenwood. An additional contingent of 40 troops was already stationed there, alongside their families, forming a small community that had flourished under the protection of the fort. However, the looming threat of the Aztecos had pushed this community to flee westward.

Scout reports indicated that a significant force of Aztecos was advancing northwest out of Congress on Highway 93, moving into what was now disputed territory. Congress, a place I remembered driving through in a seemingly different life, was now a strategic point on the map, marking the volatile frontier between The Iron Lady's domain and areas controlled by the Aztecos.

As we marched, the landscape around us was a stark reminder of the ongoing struggle for control. The barren, contested terrains were a no-man's land where safety was a luxury and survival a constant battle. Despite the unease about the coming conflict, there was a determination among the troops. This was more than just a march; it was a movement towards what could either be a significant victory or a devastating defeat.

The strategic importance of Greenwood, not just as a military outpost but as a symbol of stability for those families who had called it home, was clear. It represented a beacon of security in a world where such assurances were rare. Our mission was critical, not just in terms of military objectives, but in ensuring the continued safety and morale of those who looked to us for protection.

As we drew closer to our destination, the sense of impending confrontation grew. Each step forward was a step into increasingly dangerous territory, where the lines between friend and foe could blur in the chaos of battle. For now, our focus was on the task at hand, preparing for what lay ahead, and bracing for the challenges that would undoubtedly test our resolve and our loyalties.

Defense Strategy at Greenwood

Days 487-490 unfolded with a crescendo of tension as we reached Greenwood. The situation rapidly deteriorated with the latest scout reports indicating that the Aztecos' numbers had swelled to approximately 300 due to alliances with two additional bands. This significant increase put us at a daunting numerical disadvantage, nearly three to one, despite our technological edge.

The atmosphere at Greenwood was charged as we began immediate preparations for the impending confrontation. The soldiers, while less experienced than the seasoned veterans among us, set about constructing defensive fortifications with a grim determination. Our Stryker armored vehicles and an array of heavy weapons were our primary advantages, but the sheer number of the Aztecos posed a severe threat.

In the midst of this, The Iron Lady summoned me to the war council. Recognizing my experience in military tactics, she sought my advice on how to effectively harass and delay the Aztecos. This approach was straight out of classic U.S. Army doctrine, which advocates using light infantry tactics to engage and disrupt the enemy, buying time and causing confusion before the main engagement.

However, the challenge was evident: our troops, though brave and willing, lacked the extensive training necessary for such sophisticated maneuvers. Most had learned their skills on the fly, trained by the few veterans within our ranks who had real combat experience. This gap in training made the implementation of traditional harassment tactics risky and potentially costly.

In the war council, I outlined several strategies:

1. Ambushes along Expected Routes: By placing small, well-armed teams along the paths the Aztecos were likely to take, we could inflict casualties and slow their progress without engaging in direct, large-scale combat.

2. Hit-and-Run Tactics: Utilizing our mobility, we could strike at the edges of their forces, drawing them into chasing us, and then swiftly retreating before they could organize a response.

3. Sabotage: If possible, disrupting their supply lines or damaging any vehicles or equipment they possessed would delay their advance and reduce their effectiveness in a prolonged fight.

Each suggestion was discussed in detail, with The Iron Lady weighing the risks and potential rewards. It was clear that while our situation was precarious, there were still options available to us that could tilt the balance in our favor.

As the meeting concluded, I was tasked with organizing and leading a small unit that would carry out the first ambushes. The weight of this responsibility was heavy on my shoulders, knowing that the lives of my men and the outcome of the battle could hinge on the success of our efforts to disrupt the enemy.

Returning to the main encampment, I looked over the troops, many of whom were young and untested in battle. The determination in their eyes was clear, but so was the underlying fear. As we prepared to move out, I focused on instilling confidence in them, emphasizing the importance of discipline and alertness.

The days ahead would test us all, not just as soldiers, but as individuals fighting for survival in a world that offered no quarter.

Reflections and the Eve of Battle

Days 491-497 were heavy with the weight of impending conflict and personal reckonings. As we settled in for the night at Greenwood, my conversation with Watson forced me to confront the murky ethics of our situation. The day's strategic meetings had left me feeling ineffective, compounded by Watson's pointed critique of my earlier hesitation on the battlefield.

"You hesitated, yet you knew the price for disobedience. You jeopardized our mission here," Watson's words were harsh but not without truth. My mind replayed the moment at the ranch —the visceral act of violence that saved us but at a moral cost. "There has to be a line somewhere," I argued, more to myself than to him, grappling with the distinction between necessary evil and moral integrity.

Watson's response was curt, a reflection of his own internal conflicts. "How's Christina by the way? Or Alana, Ruslana, how about the folks you left behind in Big Bear?" His questions, though rhetorical, pierced the armor I had built around my conscience. He then silently pulled his cowboy hat over his face, signaling the end of our discussion.

As I lay down to sleep, the silence of the night was a stark contrast to the turmoil within me. Half of me resonated with Watson's pragmatism, necessary for survival in this harsh new world. Yet, the other half was disgusted by the compromises we had made, the lines we had crossed. Alexis's face haunted my thoughts, a reminder of the ideals I once held dear and how far I had strayed from them.

The unease of my conscience mingled with the strategic uncertainties of our position. Without adequate scouts or intelligence on the Aztecos' movements, we were blind in strategic terms, forced to prepare for an assault from an unknown quarter. The narrow desert valleys around Greenwood, perfect for ambushes, remained unmonitored, leaving us vulnerable and exposed.

As the night deepened, so did my reflections on the path that had led me here. The stark realization that each decision, each act of violence, had distanced me further from the man I once was. Yet, as dawn approached, bringing with it the likelihood of battle, I knew that these reflections would have to be shelved. Survival was now the immediate goal, and every soldier, every commander, would need to be unified in the face of the enemy.

The coming days promised no respite from the violence or the moral dilemmas it engendered. As I drifted into a restless sleep, I understood that the battle ahead was twofold: one for survival against the Aztecos, and another, perhaps even more daunting, against the darkness within ourselves.

The Tension Before the Storm

As the days leading up to the anticipated confrontation with the Aztecos dwindled, the atmosphere at Greenwood became increasingly charged with a tense anticipation. It's often said in the military that the waiting is worse than the combat itself. This sentiment echoed strongly in the dry, sandy expanse of the Big Sandy River, where we found ourselves making preparations.

The river, now nothing more than a wide swath of sand, offered no strategic advantage in terms of water supply or natural defense. Instead, we were positioned on a slight rise behind the dried riverbed, a location that provided a good visual over the approaching terrain but little else in terms of tactical benefit. The choice of this outpost's location was, in retrospect, questionable at best.

We worked tirelessly, filling sandbags and fortifying positions along the perimeter of the concrete cinder block outpost. The defensive setup included heavy machine guns—a .50 Cal and four M240 Bravos—strategically placed on sandbag platforms to cover the approaches. The Strykers, our most significant asset in terms of firepower, were positioned with two on each end of our line. Three were equipped with .50 caliber machine guns, and one boasted a Mark 19 automatic grenade launcher. I was particularly relieved to have the Mark 19 at our disposal; its capability to deliver a relentless barrage of explosive grenades made it an invaluable tool for area denial.

The additional trenches we constructed along our flanks were more about diligence than necessity. The open, flat terrain surrounding us provided no natural cover, making any flanking maneuvers by the enemy highly unlikely and easily detectable. Our main concern was a direct assault, which the enemy would likely attempt with sheer numbers given their lack of heavy fire support capabilities.

Each step in our preparations was driven by a mix of professional rigor and a deep-seated awareness of what was at stake. Discussions among the troops were sparse, focused, each of us perhaps contemplating the same grim calculations about the days to come. Who among us would survive, who might fall, and the impact our actions would have on the outcome of this conflict.

As night fell over the outpost, the buzz of activity gradually subsided into a tense silence. The soldiers took to their assigned posts, eyes straining in the darkness toward the horizon from which the enemy would come. The stillness was unsettling— a stark contrast to the flurry of preparation that had filled the daylight hours.

Lying in my makeshift bunk that night, the reality of our situation settled heavily upon me. Tomorrow, or the next day, we would see if our efforts could hold against the tide of an enemy driven by fervor and numbers. Tonight, though, we waited—each soldier alone with their thoughts, their fears, and their hopes. The waiting was indeed the hardest part, filled with shadows and the echoes of what might come with the dawn.

Night Before the Battle

Days 498 to 500 were consumed by an eerie tension as the sounds of the Aztecos approached. The night air was thick with the unsettling echoes of drums and a cacophony of chants, screams, and groans that reverberated across the dark desert, making the atmosphere one of impending doom. The psychological impact on our troops was palpable; the ancient and brutal war rituals of the Aztecos, enhanced by the use of powerful hallucinogens, had turned them into what seemed like supernatural warriors, capable of withstanding wounds that would normally incapacitate a man.

As I made my way to The Iron Lady's command tent, the weight of command and the responsibility for the lives of men and women under my charge pressed heavily upon me. I could see the fear and uncertainty in the eyes of our soldiers as they listened to the haunting sounds emanating from the enemy lines. It was clear that this psychological warfare was taking its toll even before the physical battle had begun.

Inside the command tent, The Iron Lady was absorbed in dispatches from various fronts, but she looked up as I entered, her expression stern yet attentive. I wasted no time in addressing the situation.

"Ma'am, our troops are under severe psychological strain from the constant noise. It's been nonstop for two days and nights. We need to counteract this demoralization," I reported, my voice laced with urgency.

The Iron Lady paused, considering the implications. "What do you suggest?" she asked, her tone indicating that she was open to practical solutions.

"We could use some of our audio equipment to play music or any kind of noise that counters the chanting. Perhaps even broadcast motivational speeches or reminders of what they're fighting for," I suggested, hoping to restore some semblance of morale and mental fortitude among the troops.

She nodded slowly, understanding the necessity of maintaining psychological as well as physical defenses. "Make it happen," she commanded, turning back to her dispatches. "Keep them focused and remind them why they hold the line."

With her approval, I exited the tent and immediately set about organizing the countermeasures. Using whatever resources we had, including loudspeakers and radio equipment, we began broadcasting a mix of uplifting music and speeches from respected leaders and veterans within our ranks. The goal was to drown out the ominous sounds of the Aztecos' rituals and to reinforce the resolve of our soldiers.

As night deepened and the first hints of dawn approached, the atmosphere among the troops shifted subtly. The music and speeches seemed to bolster their spirits, and a renewed sense of purpose took hold. They were reminded that they weren't just fighting for survival, but for a future free from the tyranny and terror that the Aztecos represented.

The preparation for battle was as much about arming the mind as it was about fortifying positions. As I checked on the defensive setups and spoke with the soldiers, reinforcing the strategic importance of their roles, I felt a grim determination settle over the camp. We were ready to face whatever came with the rising sun, united not just by fear or duty, but by a collective will to prevail.

As The Iron Lady and I discussed the morale of the troops, the tension in the tent suddenly escalated into a life-threatening situation. Just as she inquired about my perception of her leadership—a question that left me internally conflicted—I noticed a subtle movement in the shadows behind her. My military training took over instantly. Without hesitation, I pulled her behind me, using my body as a shield. The sharp hiss of darts flying through the air was followed by the thud as they embedded themselves into my armor.

Shocked but unharmed, I quickly drew my pistol. A figure emerged aggressively from the darkness of the tent's periphery. Simultaneously, a second assailant, armed with a large knife, was making a stealthy approach through a slit they had silently cut in the tent fabric. Reacting with trained precision, I fired at the first attacker, hitting him twice in the chest and once in the head as he fell to ensure he was neutralized.

Then, turning towards the second assailant, I aimed and fired two quick shots. The figure crumpled to the ground, motionless. The Iron Lady, though initially taken aback, recovered quickly and surveyed the scene with a commander's eye.

"Secure the perimeter!" she shouted, her voice cutting through the sudden chaos as she radioed for backup. Soldiers responded immediately, flooding into the tent with weapons drawn, securing the area and ensuring no further threats were present.

In the aftermath of the ambush, as the adrenaline began to subside, I checked The Iron Lady for any injuries before assessing my own condition. The darts had not penetrated my armor, but the close call was a stark reminder of the constant danger we faced—not just from the impending battle with the Aztecos but from hidden enemies who opposed her rule.

The Iron Lady, composed yet clearly shaken by the attempt on her life, turned to me with a nod of gratitude. "It seems you are not just an advisor but a guardian as well," she said, her tone mixed with respect and a newfound wariness of her vulnerability.

As we awaited the all-clear from the security team, the gravity of the situation settled in. The attack within what was supposed to be a secure command post highlighted the internal threats that could be just as deadly as the external ones. It was a harsh reminder that in this new world, vigilance was as crucial as valor.

This incident solidified my role not only as a tactical advisor but as a key protector within the ranks, deeply intertwined with the safety and stability of our leadership. As we prepared to address the troops, the need for a unifying speech was more apparent than ever—not only to bolster morale but to reinforce solidarity in the face of all forms of adversity.

Encounter with the Matadors

Days 501 brought chaos and fear to the fore as the camp reeled from the sudden ambush and the eerie aftermath. The slain attackers, referred to as 'matadors' by Evan, lay grotesquely disfigured on the ground, their bodies scarred and modified to blend seamlessly with the desert environment. Their appearance was unsettling—a stark manifestation of the Aztecos' brutal and mystical practices.

The matadors wore only sandy brown loincloths and had their teeth blackened and sharpened to points, evoking images of predatory animals. The patterns of raised scars covering their bodies mimicked natural textures, making them almost invisible in the desert until it was too late. Evan explained that these men were not just warriors but symbols of fear and power, designed to intimidate as much as to fight.

As we surveyed the damage and reassessed our defenses, the sound of the Strykers' .50 caliber machine guns erupted, slicing through the tense silence of the night. Other troops shouted commands, trying to coordinate a response to unseen threats lurking in the darkness. The surreal wailing that rose from the desert sent shivers down the spine, a psychological tactic employed by the Aztecos to unnerve their foes before an assault.

The camp was a hive of activity, with soldiers scrambling to man their positions and reinforce vulnerable points in our defenses. The realization that we were up against an enemy that embraced both ancient rituals and modern guerrilla tactics made the threat all the more dire.

In this heightened state of alert, everyone knew that the true battle had yet to begin. The Aztecos had announced their presence not just with their chilling cries but with a direct challenge to our preparedness and resolve. As dawn approached, the tension was palpable, with every soldier braced for the onslaught that seemed inevitable.

The night's events had hardened our resolve but also deepened our understanding of the enemy. These were no ordinary fighters; they were the embodiment of their tribe's fierce and mystical heritage, warriors who transformed fear into a weapon as potent as any firearm.

As we stood ready, watching the dark horizon, I knew that the coming daylight would bring more than just light—it would usher in a test of our courage, our strategy, and our very survival. The camp, once a place of organized military strength, now felt like the frontline of a much darker conflict, where warfare was as much about battling fear and superstition as it was about defeating the enemy in combat.

CHAPTER 3: THE ONSLAUGHT OF THE AZTECOS

Days 600 marked a turning point as the full force of the Azteco army bore down on us. The Iron Lady, undeterred by the night's assassination attempt, donned her combat gear with a vigor that belied the danger we faced. Her command presence was undeniable, issuing orders with a sharp clarity that galvanized her troops. It was in this moment, amidst the chaos, that her leadership shone—unwavering and fearless.

As we settled into the central position on the outer perimeter, the advancing horde of Aztecos became visible. They weren't just a few hundred as intelligence had suggested, but appeared to be thousands strong. The ground seemed to shake with their approach, a human tidal wave of screaming warriors rushing toward us across the desert plain.

The Iron Lady's strategy was clear and deliberate. "Save your rifles until they're within 200 meters. Let the .50 caliber machine guns do their work until then. The Jaguar Warriors, their frontline infantry, are bullet sponges. The real attack is behind them," she commanded. Her troops adjusted quickly, focusing the heavy machine guns on the approaching wave.

These Jaguar Warriors, so named by the Aztecos, were a terrifying sight. Armed with primitive weapons like clubs, spears, and makeshift axes, they charged with a ferocity that was both awe-inspiring and horrifying. More disturbing was their apparent disregard for their own lives, driven by a potent cocktail of drugs that induced a psychotic state, making them virtually immune to pain.

Our machine guns roared to life, tearing through the ranks of the Jaguar Warriors with brutal efficiency. Yet, for every warrior that fell, another seemed to take his place, undeterred, continuing their mad charge towards our defenses. It was a macabre dance of death, where the ancient clashed with the modern in a grim ballet of warfare.

The Iron Lady stood resolute at the front lines, rifle in hand, her eyes scanning the battlefield with a strategic mind that assessed every move and countermove. Her presence bolstered the morale of her troops, reminding them of the stakes at play— not just for survival, but for the future of the territory under her control.

As the Jaguar Warriors closed the distance, the sound of our rifles joined the cacophony of machine gun fire. The battle became a desperate struggle, each shot aimed with the hope of holding back the tide of warriors who seemed innumerable and inexhaustible.

In these moments, the true nature of war was laid bare—a chaotic, brutal affair where strategy met primal savagery. The Iron Lady's leadership was a beacon in this storm, guiding her troops through the onslaught with a tactical acumen that commanded respect, even in the heart of battle. As the enemy drew closer, every soldier knew that the fight was far from over, and that their resolve would be tested to its utmost limits.

As the battle raged on, the Aztecos unleashed their Jaguar Warriors in a full sprint across the 400 meters of sandy expanse that lay before the banks of the now dry Big Sandy River. Their incredible speed and lack of fear were unnerving, as they closed the distance with relentless fury, their war cries chilling the air.

Our Striker vehicles, armed with heavy .50 caliber machine guns, tore through the advancing lines with brutal efficiency. The rounds were devastating, severing limbs and creating gruesome wounds. Yet, astonishingly, some of the Jaguar Warriors continued their charge, driven by sheer adrenaline or the potent drugs in their systems, managing several more strides before collapsing lifelessly onto the sand.

Behind the frenzied front line, the real threat emerged. The Aztecos' archers, known as 'acueros', followed. These were not the primitive fighters of the front lines but well-trained infantry equipped with modern firearms. In a war where ammunition was becoming a scarce resource, these soldiers were conservatively using their firepower, a strategic reserve force that added a lethal layer to their assault.

Amidst the chaos, I noticed two streaks of light arching through the sky from behind the Aztecos' lines. My heart sank as I realized what they were—Javelin anti-tank missiles. Known for their devastating effectiveness, these missiles had been a decisive factor in modern conflicts around the globe.

It was too late to warn the Striker crews. In less than ten seconds from launch, two of our Strikers were hit. The impact was catastrophic. The missiles' warheads, designed to defeat heavy armor, made short work of the Strikers' relatively thin protection. The vehicles erupted into flames, the explosion sending deadly shrapnel flying, which caused additional casualties among the nearby soldiers.

The loss of the Strikers was a significant blow to our defensive capabilities. Not only had we lost valuable firepower, but the psychological impact of seeing such powerful assets destroyed so swiftly was demoralizing.

As the smoke from the destroyed Strikers billowed into the night sky, the Aztecos seized the moment, their acueros moving up under the cover of the chaos to take more strategic positions. The battlefield shifted with each passing second, becoming more perilous as the enemy exploited our sudden weakness.

In the heat of battle, with adrenaline coursing through my veins, I realized that each decision now could mean the difference between life and death. The command structure had to adapt quickly, rallying the troops and reorganizing our lines to prevent a complete rout.

The fighting grew more intense, a brutal clash of modern tactics and primal ferocity. As the commander on the ground, my focus sharpened. The battle was far from over, and despite the setback, our resolve hardened. We would regroup, respond, and hold our ground, for retreat was not an option. The fight for survival was on, and every soldier, every weapon, every tactic would count in the harrowing hours to come.

The Melee at the Perimeter

The battlefield was in utter chaos as the relentless Jaguars continued their frenzied charge toward our defensive positions. With only one Striker remaining on our right flank, equipped with a Mark 19 automatic grenade launcher, we had a momentary upper hand. The Striker unleashed a barrage of

40mm grenades, each explosion creating a deadly radius that tore through the tightly packed ranks of the enemy. Yet, despite the devastating losses, the Jaguars' advance seemed unstoppable, their fanaticism undiminished by the heavy casualties.

As they closed into engagement range, I raised my rifle, following The Iron Lady's orders to conserve ammunition and ensure more accurate shots at closer distances. The strategy was sound, maximizing the effectiveness of our firepower, but it allowed the enemy dangerously close to our positions.

The air was thick with the smell of gunpowder and blood as Jaguar after Jaguar was cut down by precise rifle and machine gun fire. But their sheer numbers and the ferocity of their assault overwhelmed our defensive efforts. In moments, the human wave of Jaguars breached our lines, surging into the defensive fighting positions where I and other soldiers were stationed.

The close quarters combat was brutal and immediate. One Jaguar, a particularly gruesome sight with half his teeth sharpened into fangs and blades attached to his arms with wires, lunged at me. The confined space made it impossible to use my rifle effectively for shooting, so I wielded it like a club instead. I blocked his slashing attack and countered with a heavy strike to his head with the butt of my rifle, knocking him backward and momentarily stunning him.

Seizing the moment, I drew my knife from my boot and plunged it into his chest. The Jaguar gasped and fell, his life ebbing away on the sandy ground. The melee continued around me, every soldier engaged in desperate hand-to-hand combat.

The intensity of the battle only increased as more Jaguars poured into our lines. We fought back fiercely, defending our position with everything we had. The sound of gunfire, shouts of soldiers, and the cries of the wounded filled the air, creating a cacophony of war that was both terrifying and exhilarating.

Throughout this dire melee, The Iron Lady's presence was a rallying point for us all. Her fearless leadership and strategic acumen under such extreme conditions inspired us to keep fighting, to hold our ground against the overwhelming odds.

As the battle raged on, each soldier knew the stakes were higher than ever. We were not just fighting for survival but for the future of our lands and our people. The enemy at our doorstep was not just a military force but a manifestation of a brutal, unyielding ideology that sought to overrun us completely.

In those desperate moments, the line between victory and defeat was razor-thin, each act of bravery and each sacrifice shaping the outcome of this pivotal clash.

Last Stand at Greenwood

As the battle at Greenwood reached its zenith, chaos reigned. Despite a mortal wound, one of the Jaguars continued his frenzied assault until he finally collapsed, lifeless. In that instant, another enemy attacked from behind, but before he could strike me fatally, The Iron Lady intervened. With precise shots from her handgun, she downed the spear-wielding Jaguar just as he was about to overrun me.

Scrambling to my feet, the harsh reality of the battlefield was laid bare as our M240 gunner was brutally struck down. Seizing the initiative, I took control of the machine gun, unleashing a barrage of fire toward the advancing horde. Amidst the relentless gunfire, a vehicle—a battered old Army Humvee— raced through the desert dust towards us, screeching to a halt nearby.

"It's hopeless! There's too many! We gotta get you out of here!" the driver shouted frantically through the open window. The Iron Lady hesitated, her instincts torn between her duty to lead and the stark reality of our situation. Despite her initial reluctance, the tactical necessity of retreat was undeniable. The driver was right; we were overwhelmed, and further resistance might lead to total annihilation.

"Everyone, out of the hole! Into the vehicle, now!" The Iron Lady commanded, her voice cutting through the din of battle. Members of her inner circle, those still able to move, scrambled towards the safety of the Humvee.

I remained behind, gripping the machine gun. "Soldier, fall back!" The Iron Lady's command was sharp, urgent.

"No, if I get off this gun, we're all dead before we reach the Humvee. Go!" I responded, steadfast. The Iron Lady, her expression grim and resolute, acknowledged with a nod and sprinted back to the vehicle. The Humvee's tires spun furiously, kicking up clouds of dust as it began its retreat.

Alone at the gun, I saw a potential break in the relentless waves of Jaguar warriors. Perhaps their main assault was finally waning, but that left the acueros—their archers—to contend with. The barrel of the M240 glowed ominously in the night from the heat of sustained firing.

As I continued to hold the line, providing critical covering fire for the retreat, the stark silhouette of the Humvee faded into the distance, a cloud of dust marking its desperate escape. I knew then that the battle for Greenwood was lost, but not all hope was extinguished. Each round I fired was a defiance of the odds, a testament to the resolve of those unwilling to yield even in the face of overwhelming adversity.

The night air was thick with the acrid smell of gunpowder and the metallic scent of blood. As the last of the Jaguars fell before my sustained fire, I prepared for the final stand. The enemy's numbers had dwindled, but so had our chances of survival. This was no longer about victory; it was about fighting with honor and defending our ground to the last.

Recovery and Reflection

Days 541-544 were spent in the blur of recovery as I gradually regained consciousness in a fully functioning hospital, a rarity in these tumultuous times. The hum of electric lights and the steady beeping of a heart monitor provided a stark contrast to the chaotic battlefield memories that still haunted my dreams.

After an unsuccessful attempt to rise from bed, which nearly ended with me collapsing to the floor, a nurse quickly came to my aid, her swift actions a reminder of my fragile state. It wasn't long before I lost consciousness again, succumbing to the exhaustion and pain that enveloped me.

When I next awoke, the familiar face of Christina greeted me. Her presence was comforting, a tangible link to a life before the war that seemed more like a distant dream now. As she held my hand, the doctor explained the extent of my injuries. A bullet, fortunately rendered less lethal by a faulty cartridge, had struck my head, causing severe bruising to my brain but not penetrating the skull. The impact had been enough to knock me unconscious and warrant a medically induced coma to allow my brain to heal without further distress.

Ben Watson, my steadfast comrade, had been the one to drag

me to safety amidst the chaos of the overrun battlefield. The Iron Lady had managed to dispatch additional vehicles to rescue survivors, but only a handful, about two dozen from over a hundred, had survived. The rest were either dead or captured, likely subjected to the horrific blood rituals that fueled the Aztecos' ferocity.

As I lay in the hospital, the reality of our defeat and the high cost of the battle settled heavily upon me. Despite the comfort of modern amenities like electricity, the weight of loss and the uncertainty of the future were ever-present.

Word reached me that The Iron Lady had requested to see me as soon as I was able to stand. Her leadership and the survival of her regime, now more than ever, depended on the loyalty and recovery of her few remaining forces. The upcoming meeting with her was not just a formality but a critical juncture to discuss the next steps in a war that had taken a dire turn.

In the quiet of the hospital room, with Christina by my side, I began to mentally prepare for what lay ahead. The battle might have been lost, but the war was far from over. The resilience to fight on, to rebuild, and to face the next challenges was kindled by the very trials that had nearly claimed my life. As I regained my strength, the determination to return to the fray grew stronger, fueled by a renewed sense of purpose and the unwavering desire to never succumb to the darkness that had enveloped our world.

Strategy and Summons

Days 545 to 549 marked a period of uneasy calm after the brutal clash at Greenwood. The visit from Watson, who had just returned from a patrol, brought a mix of news. While the Aztecos had pulled back from their aggressive push, their retreat did little to alleviate the tension that hung over us. Watson described it as the ominous stillness that often precedes a severe storm, his words echoing the sentiment of impending doom that seemed to shadow the temporary peace.

My stay in the hospital continued as the doctors wanted to ensure no lingering complications from the head injury. Despite the sporadic headaches that clouded my thoughts, I felt a growing urgency to return to my duties. The world outside the hospital walls was moving on, and I needed to be part of it.

After a couple of days recuperating at home with Christina, a summons from The Iron Lady abruptly pulled me back into the fold. The message was clear and immediate: I was to report to her headquarters without delay. With a mixture of apprehension and resolve, I made my way to her command center, escorted by two of her guards.

Upon arrival, I found The Iron Lady, Evan, deep in consultation with her top military advisors. They were huddled around a large map sprawled across a table, which depicted her vast territories and the known positions of enemy forces. The room was tense, with the air thick with the weight of crucial decisions being made.

As the meeting concluded, Evan's sharp gaze cut across the room to me, signaling me to approach. The map in front of her was dotted with markers and notes, a visual representation of the precarious balance of power her army maintained.

"Thank you for coming," she began, her voice steady despite the obvious exhaustion that lined her features. "We're at a critical juncture. The Aztecos have retreated, but we both know it's temporary. They're regrouping, and we must use this time wisely."

She pointed to several locations on the map where scout reports had indicated possible Azteco movements. "Our patrols have kept them at bay, but we can't rely on skirmishes to deter a full-scale assault. We need a robust strategy to secure our defenses and consider possible counterattacks."

The Iron Lady's strategy involved reinforcing vulnerable points along the perimeter of her territory and increasing surveillance to detect any early signs of another Azteco advance. She also planned to send out diplomatic envoys to nearby settlements to solidify alliances and gather more support.

As she outlined her plans, it was clear she was preparing not just to defend but also to take the initiative if necessary. "I need you back in command," she stated firmly, looking me directly in the eyes. "Your experience and leadership on the front lines are invaluable."

The gravity of her words and the weight of the responsibility she was entrusting me with felt both daunting and invigorating. As I nodded in agreement, ready to take on the tasks ahead, I knew that the coming days would be filled with challenges. But with the trust of The Iron Lady and the support of seasoned soldiers like Watson, I was prepared to face whatever the future held, determined to stand firm against the storm on the horizon.

Uncertainty and Ceremony

As we stood over the map of her territories, The Iron Lady and I scrutinized the missing blue pin at Greenwood and other fortifications along the border, each marked by empty pinholes. "They've hit across a wide front in the last month," I noted, pointing out the pattern of engagements that hinted at the Aztecos' tactics but did not indicate a clear strategy for territorial control.

"It could be they're probing our defenses, learning how we fight and what we have," I suggested, analyzing the situation. "Or, it might be a diversionary tactic, aiming to fix our forces here in the east while planning a larger assault from another direction—south would be my guess."

The Iron Lady nodded in agreement, her expression contemplative. "I've got scouts out north and south, looking for any signs of a main force," she replied. "So far, they haven't seen anything substantial. We're not reinforcing the lost outposts yet, not until we're certain where the main attack will come from." Her strategy was clear—conserve resources and avoid spreading our defenses too thin until more information could be gathered.

As we concluded our strategic discussion, The Iron Lady cleared her throat and motioned for me to follow her outside. We stepped into a small courtyard that had once served as a relaxation area for city workers. Now, it had been transformed under her command into a sort of ceremonial gathering place. A small crowd had already assembled, their faces turning towards me with expressions of respect and anticipation.

I felt a mix of curiosity and apprehension as I stood there, waiting for what was to come. The Iron Lady took her place at the front, signaling the beginning of the ceremony. She began to speak, her voice carrying clearly over the heads of those gathered.

"Today, we recognize the bravery and sacrifice of those who have stood against the Aztecos," she announced, her gaze occasionally returning to me. "In recognition of his valor and crucial role in our recent battles, and his undeniable impact on our survival, we are here to honor one of our own."

The crowd's eyes were on me, and a murmur of approval ran through them as The Iron Lady continued, "For his leadership and bravery, and for his strategic acumen that has saved many lives, we present this commendation."

A young aide stepped forward, holding a small, ornate box which The Iron Lady took and opened, revealing a medal of honor. She stepped towards me, pinning the medal onto my uniform. The weight of the metal felt heavy on my chest, not just in its physical presence but in the responsibility it symbolized.

The ceremony, though brief, was poignant, highlighting not only personal recognition but the collective resilience of those fighting under The Iron Lady's command. As the applause rang out, I felt a renewed sense of duty and determination. The war was far from over, and the path ahead was fraught with uncertainty, but this moment of acknowledgment reminded all present that courage and leadership were our greatest assets in the face of such overwhelming odds.

Honor and Consequence

As The Iron Lady ascended a small raised platform to address the assembled crowd, the gravity of the moment weighed heavily upon me. She spoke eloquently of the recent battle, acknowledging our losses and vowing revenge against our enemies. The crowd listened intently, their emotions palpable in the silent pauses of her speech.

When she turned her attention to me, the air seemed to thicken. "For heroism covering the retreat of myself and my command staff under the threat of certain death, I award you the First

Sun, one of our highest honors." Her words echoed across the plaza, and all eyes were on me. The honor was significant, yet it was a surreal moment; I had never imagined receiving such recognition, especially not from a leader known for commanding an army with questionable ethics.

The medal she pinned on me was distinct—a raised fist defiantly thrust into the sky, a symbol of resistance and strength. The craftsmanship was meticulous, indicating that it wasn't just an artifact from before the war but something created with purpose under her rule.

After the award, The Iron Lady's expression shifted as she reminded the crowd—and me—of the gravity of military discipline. "However, you still defied a direct order to retreat. In light of your heroism and self-sacrifice, I am commuting your sentence from death to 20 lashes." The stark juxtaposition of honor with punishment sent a clear message about the complexities of leadership and the harsh realities of martial law.

Led to a clearing in the plaza, I approached a large wooden pole equipped with restraints, a grim reminder of the consequences of my actions. The pole, clearly used often, stood as a symbol of order and discipline within her ranks. As I approached, Robert, a trusted comrade, was there to meet me. His presence was both a comfort and a solemn reminder of the duty we owed to each other and to those we led.

I faced the crowd, my expression stoic. The recognition of my actions brought pride, but the impending punishment was a humbling reminder of the cost of leadership and the burden of command. As I was secured to the pole, I felt a mix of emotions —pride for what I had achieved and a deep sense of introspection about the path that had led me here.

The lashes were delivered in quick succession, each strike a sharp reminder of the fine line between heroism and insubordination. The pain was sharp, but my resolve did not waver. I understood that in this new world, leadership demanded not just the courage to fight but also the strength to bear the consequences of one's decisions.

As the final lash was struck, I was released from the pole, my back raw and burning, but my spirit undeterred. The crowd, which had watched in silent respect, now offered their nods and murmurs of approval, not just for the honor I had received but for accepting the punishment with dignity.

This moment, painful yet proud, was a defining one. It underscored the complex dynamics of power, loyalty, and discipline that shaped our lives amid the chaos of a world remade by relentless conflict. As I walked away from the pole, the weight of the medal on my chest was a constant reminder of the burdens and honors of leadership.

Recovery and Reflections

Days 550-554 were spent in quiet convalescence at home, the stark contrast of the bustling hospital now replaced by the solemnity of recovery in familiar surroundings. Christina was by my side, her presence a comforting constant as I navigated the physical pain and emotional tumult following the public whipping.

Christina's emotions were raw; her eyes often brimming with tears of frustration and anger. "She had you whipped," she repeated, the words thick with emotion. It was difficult for her to reconcile the respect and recognition I had received with the harshness of the punishment that followed.

I tried to explain, carefully choosing my words. "It's their way of maintaining order, of showing that even those who are honored are not above the law. It was both a punishment and a lesson—a reminder that in the ranks, discipline must prevail."

Christina listened, her expression a mix of understanding and skepticism. "But at such a cost?" she questioned, her voice a whisper. "To be honored and then humiliated in front of those... those people."

I sighed, the complexity of the situation not lost on me. "It's a delicate balance. The Iron Lady uses these moments to reinforce her authority and the rule of law, no matter how harsh it may seem. It's not just about punishment; it's about setting an example. And despite everything, it was also a protection—it could have been much worse without her intervention."

The days passed with Christina tending to my wounds, her care meticulous and gentle. Each bandage change was a quiet reminder of the ordeal, yet it also marked the healing not just of physical scars, but of understanding the burden of leadership and the cost of decisions in a world ruled by power and survival.

As my strength returned, so did our conversations about the future. "What will you do now?" Christina asked one evening, the question hanging in the air like the cool night breeze through the open window.

I looked at her, my resolve firming. "I will continue to serve. There's much to be done, and if I can influence things for the better, even in small ways, then everything I've endured will have been worth it."

Christina nodded, her hand finding mine, squeezing it with a strength that spoke of shared burdens and shared hopes. "Then I'll be here, with you. But promise me, no more secrets. No more holding back the dangers of what you face out there."

I promised, knowing full well the road ahead would be fraught with challenges. But with Christina's support, and the recognition of both the honor and the weight of my role within the army, I felt ready to face whatever came next. The lessons learned were not just about surviving the battle but about understanding the deeper battles waged within the ranks and within oneself.

Evan entered the room with the poise of a leader accustomed to crisis, her gaze sweeping the room before settling on me. Her presence was commanding, yet there was an underlying weariness that perhaps only those close to her could detect.

Christina's polite nod barely masked her turmoil as she excused herself, the sound of her footsteps receding upstairs spoke volumes more than words could. Watson, meanwhile, resettled into his seat, his earlier alertness transitioning back to his usual guarded relaxation, pipe in hand.

"I hope I'm not interrupting," Evan began, her tone acknowledging the obvious strain in the room. She looked towards the stairs Christina had ascended before turning back to me, her expression softening slightly. "I wanted to see how you were healing, but it seems I've come at a tense time."

I nodded, appreciative of her concern yet mindful of the complexities her presence brought into our home. "Recovery is going well, thanks to Christina's care," I replied, gesturing towards the staircase, indicating Christina's significant role in my recuperation

Evan acknowledged this with a nod, then her gaze turned more serious. "I understand this isn't easy—for any of you. The honors we bestowed were well earned, yet I know the price was high. Not just physically." Her eyes met mine, a leader's resolve mingling with empathetic understanding.

Watson, observing our exchange, took a thoughtful puff from his pipe before interjecting, "The path we've chosen isn't without its thorns, but it's the one we believe in. That counts for something."

Evan agreed, "It does. And it's why I'm here, not just to check on your recovery, but to discuss what comes next." She paused, ensuring she had my full attention. "We're at a pivotal moment. The Aztecos are regrouping, and we need to be ready. Your insight has proven invaluable, and we need that moving forward."

The room filled with a heavy silence, each of us contemplating the weight of her words and the challenges that lay ahead. Evan's visit was not merely a courtesy call; it was a summons back to the responsibilities awaiting outside the comfort of recovery.

"I'll be ready," I assured her, feeling the truth of the statement bolstered by the support of those around me, despite the underlying tensions.

Evan nodded, satisfied with my response, her demeanor shifting as she prepared to leave, signaling the end of her visit. "Take the time you need, but remember, the sooner we can have you back, the better."

With a final nod to Watson and a respectful acknowledgment of the space Christina had retreated to, Evan departed, leaving us to absorb the implications of her visit. Watson broke the silence, a wry chuckle escaping him as he remarked, "Well, it's never dull around here, is it?"

I managed a smile, despite the complexity of emotions. "No, it certainly isn't." The reality was clear: recovery time was almost over, and the demands of the war awaited. The brief respite at home had been a necessary pause, but the road ahead required a return to the fray, with all its inherent dangers and decisions.

flaws, you've seen the necessity of its existence. We protect not just against the chaos within but against a far greater evil without."

The Iron Lady paused, letting her words sink in as she finished applying the salve. Her touch was clinical but not devoid of compassion—a complex leader, a pragmatist who acknowledged the brutal nature of her command yet sought to instill a semblance of order amidst chaos.

"You're sending me back to California?" I asked, the reality of her proposal dawning on me. It was an unexpected turn, but it made sense. She needed an ambassador, someone who had witnessed firsthand the harshness and the necessity of her rule and could explain it to those who were spared the direct impact.

"Yes," she confirmed, wiping her hands on a cloth. "You understand what we're fighting against. You've seen what happens when the aztecos overrun territories. We need the settlements in the west to understand the threat at their door. They need to be prepared, maybe even align with us for mutual protection."

The strategy was clear. The Iron Lady wasn't just fighting for her territory; she was looking to build a coalition, recognizing that isolated communities, no matter how free, would stand little chance against organized hordes like the Aztecos.

"Take your time to recover," she advised, stepping back to look me in the eye. "But when you're ready, I need you to take our message. Show them the stakes. Help them understand why we fight so hard, why our methods, though severe, are necessary."

Her gaze was steady, her resolve clear. This was not just a mission; it was a plea for unity in the face of a common enemy. As she left, her parting words lingered in the air, a reminder of the weight now placed upon my shoulders.

Watson, ever the silent observer during these exchanges, finally spoke up, his voice low. "It's a heavy burden, carrying truth to those who might not want to hear it. But maybe, just maybe, it'll save more lives than we know."

I sat there, absorbing the depth of my new mission. It was a daunting task, but necessary. If anything, my time with the Army of the Dawn had taught me that sometimes, the lesser of two evils was not only a choice but a necessity. With the Iron Lady's salve cooling the physical wounds on my back, I prepared mentally for the challenge ahead. Returning home would not just be a reunion, but a crucial step in fortifying the west against the encroaching darkness.

Preparations and Departure

Days 555 to 560 were spent in a flurry of preparations, despite my physical limitations. The silence left in the wake of The Iron Lady's departure was palpable, heavy with implications and responsibilities. Watson and I busied ourselves with the practical aspects of my forthcoming journey back to California, a task that helped distract from the weightier considerations of alliances and threats.

Christina, meanwhile, maintained a distance, her demeanor reflective and reserved. She was unaware of my past life with Alexis, and I felt the gap between us widen as I withheld parts of my history, focusing instead on the immediate future.

As the days passed, Christina's reluctance for me to leave before fully recovering became more evident. "You're not ready to go back out there," she implored, her concern palpable. "You need more time to heal."

I understood her fears, but the urgency of The Iron Lady's mission pressed on me. "I know, Christina, but the sooner we get the word out and start preparing, the better our chances. The Aztecos won't wait for me to heal."

By days 561 to 564, my departure was imminent. Christina helped me pack, her movements slow and deliberate, each item a silent testament to her conflicted feelings. "Please, just wait a bit longer," she pleaded one evening as she folded clothes next to my half-packed bag.

"I can't," I responded gently. "The threat is real, and we need to act. I'll be careful, I promise." Her eyes, filled with a mix of fear and resignation, met mine, and in them, I saw the burden of my choices weigh on her too.

On the morning of my departure, Watson helped me with the heavier items, ensuring that I wouldn't strain myself. The Iron Lady's orders were clear: travel light, move fast, and gather support. She had provided a requisition chit for supplies from the Armory—lightweight armor, a reliable sidearm, extra ammunition, and a few essentials for survival in the wasteland.

Christina stood by the doorway as I adjusted the straps on my backpack. Her hands were clasped tightly in front of her, the tension in her posture betraying her attempt at composure. I stepped closer, pulling her into a brief, tight embrace. "I'll be back before you know it," I murmured, trying to offer comfort with words that felt woefully inadequate.

She nodded, her voice barely a whisper. "Just come back to me. That's all I ask."

With a final look at the home we had shared, I stepped out into the early morning light, Watson at my side. We made our way to the vehicle that would take us to the edge of the territory, where the real journey would begin. As we drove away, I couldn't help but feel the weight of every look and word exchanged with Christina. It wasn't just a physical journey that lay ahead—it was one that would test the resilience of bonds formed in the shadow of war.

Journey and Reflections

Days 565 to 570 were marked by the rhythmic cadence of travel, the road unfolding before us like a ribbon through the wasteland. As we made camp each evening, the crackle of the campfire became our sanctuary from the relentless march. One evening, as we shared tales and observations, I joked about feeling as if I'd been on the road since the world ended. The laughter that followed was genuine, a rare moment of levity that pierced the usual pall of our grim mission.

Traveling with Watson and Christina, I couldn't help but reflect on the paths that had led each of us here. The last few months under The Iron Lady's command had forced us into corners of our own morality we had never anticipated visiting. The deeds we had committed in the name of survival and security weighed heavily on us, binding us together not just in purpose but also in shared culpability.

It was hard to admit, but part of me wondered if we belonged to the Army of the Dawn more than we ever would back in the more peaceful, if naive, West. Christina, who had come into her own harshly in the crucible of this new world, had killed only to protect me. That night changed her, and although it forged a rift between us, it also tied us more tightly together. She was vigilant, always on the edge, a stark contrast to the woman she had been before the world fell apart.

As I lay down beside her each night, the space between us filled with the crackling of the fire, I couldn't help but let my mind wander to what peace might look like, if we could ever find it. Guilt washed over me as my thoughts invariably drifted from Christina to Alexis, the past mingling with the present in the quiet moments before sleep claimed me.

Days 571 to 575 continued in a similar vein, with each day blending into the next, marked only by the changing scenery and the occasional encounter with other travelers—each wary and tired, like us. We shared what news we could, piecing together a picture of the world that seemed both vast and trapped in endless conflict.

One evening, as we sat looking out over a particularly desolate stretch of the wasteland, Christina turned to me, her voice low. "Do you ever think about what we'll do if we actually make it back? If we bring everyone together?"

I looked at her, struck by the hope in her voice, mingled with uncertainty. "Every day," I replied honestly. "I think about it all the time. And I wonder if we can ever really go back to how things were, or if we're just forging a new path that looks nothing like the past."

The conversation lingered in the air, mingling with the smoke from the fire, as we each considered our future in a world that demanded so much and offered so little certainty. The journey was far from over, but each step brought us closer not just to our destination, but to understanding the true cost of the world we were fighting to save—or perhaps to create anew.

Encounters at the Border

Days 575 to 579 brought us into contact with the harsh realities of border control under The Iron Lady's regime. As we approached one of the fortified checkpoints that marked the boundary of her territory, we witnessed a distressing scene: a caravan of refugees being turned away by the border guards.

The group consisted mostly of families from the western reaches of The Iron Lady's kingdom, each person's face etched with fear and uncertainty. They had likely heard rumors or had firsthand experiences of the Aztecos' brutality and were desperate to find safety in the far west. However, instead of assistance or empathy, they were met with hostility and threats from the guards, who were aggressively enforcing The Iron Lady's directive to prevent mass exodus from her lands.

Watson, Christina, and I watched as the guards shouted at the huddled masses, brandishing their clubs with menacing authority. "Move back! No passage!" one of the guards yelled, his voice carrying across the tense air.

This blockade was not just about maintaining population control or preventing the spread of panic; it was also a show of power, a reminder that within her borders, The Iron Lady's word was law. The refugees, having nowhere else to go, reluctantly started to disband, their hopes of escape dashed as they turned their vehicles around under the watchful eyes of the guards.

"Should we do something?" Christina whispered, her voice tight with emotion.

I shook my head slightly. "There's nothing we can do right now," I murmured back. "This is bigger than us."

The reality of the situation was grim. The Iron Lady's policies might have been designed to maintain order and security within her territories, but they also trapped innocent people in a region increasingly threatened by external horrors.

As we moved past the checkpoint, continuing our journey westward, the image of the frightened families stayed with us. The encounter served as a sobering reminder of the complexities of leadership in a post-apocalyptic world. It wasn't just about defending against external threats but also about managing the internal dynamics of a frightened population.

In the following days, our conversations often circled back to what we had witnessed. The moral dilemmas presented by The Iron Lady's rule were complex. On one hand, her strict policies could be seen as necessary to prevent chaos and preserve resources; on the other, they smacked of tyranny, punishing those who merely sought safety.

As we set up camp on the evening of day 579, the weight of our experiences hung heavy around the fire. We were silent for a long time, each lost in thought, pondering the role we were playing in this broader conflict. Was there a right answer? Could there be any peace when so much of the world was governed by fear?

These questions lingered as the fire crackled before us, the flames casting long shadows over our makeshift camp. The road ahead was uncertain, and as we continued our journey, it was clear that the challenges we would face were as much moral as they were physical.

Journey Beyond Borders

Days 580 to 585 marked a significant transition as we finally crossed the frontier of The Iron Lady's dominion. The guard captain at the border, upon seeing the orders I carried, hesitated initially but ultimately did not obstruct our passage. He was a man caught between duty and pragmatism, aware that any misstep in dealing with The Iron Lady's direct commands could lead to severe repercussions for him.

As we ventured beyond the confines of her rule, the stark dichotomies of her governance remained a topic of intense discussion among us. Just outside her territory, we encountered another caravan, this one heading towards her lands. It was a scavenging mission, evident from the loaded wagons of supplies, but chillingly, it included a group of survivors bound together by ropes around their necks. These individuals were not volunteers; they were captives, likely destined for servitude under The Iron Lady's rule.

Christina turned her face away, unable to watch. Watson and I shared a look, his eyes probing mine for reassurance or perhaps doubt. I felt a deep discomfort stirring within me, torn between the relative stability provided by The Iron Lady and the undeniable harshness of her methods.

As we moved farther from her territory, the discussions around the campfire grew more philosophical. "Was this really the only way?" Christina asked one evening, her voice low, filled with a mix of fear and resignation. "Is this what it takes to rebuild the world from ashes?"

I mulled over her question, recalling The Iron Lady's justification: granting the raiders and cannibals certain freedoms was a necessary evil to maintain control and gradually steer them towards civilization. "She believes that over time, as stability returns, the need for such brutal tactics will diminish," I explained, though my own conviction wavered.

Days 586 to 590 found us navigating through landscapes that were both physically and morally desolate. We encountered other travelers and remnants of communities along the way, each interaction providing a glimpse into the myriad ways humanity was adapting to the new world. Some had chosen isolation, others formed tight-knit, guarded communities, and some had fallen into anarchy.

As we set up camp on the evening of day 590, the reality of our mission weighed heavily upon us. We were messengers bearing not just news of the external threats looming over the horizon but also of the internal compromises some believed necessary to face such threats.

"Our role isn't to judge," Watson said as we sat around the fire, "but to inform. People deserve to make their own choices about their future, based on all the facts."

Christina nodded, her expression somber. "And perhaps in sharing what we know, we'll find others who believe there's a better way, one that doesn't require such harsh compromises."

That night, as I lay under the stars, I pondered the complexity of rebuilding civilization in a world where the old moral compasses no longer pointed true north. The journey ahead was not just about traversing physical distances but about bridging ideological divides, understanding different visions for the future, and confronting the question of what sacrifices were truly necessary for the rebirth of society.

Return to Farmbridge

Days 596 to 600 brought us closer to Farmbridge, with every step intensifying the mix of anticipation and uncertainty about our return. Ruslana had clearly been preparing; her scouts, unfamiliar faces to me, met us with a cautious but guided approach, leading us through safer paths that skirted around the dangers of Slab City to the north. Watson's silent nod confirmed my thoughts: Farmbridge was expanding, becoming more than just a small settlement, a testament to Ruslana's leadership.

Yet, as we neared the gates of Farmbridge, my mind wrestled with the dilemma of what to share. The reality of the Aztecos' threat and The Iron Lady's offer of an alliance — these were truths that could alter the fate of this community I had grown to care deeply about. Could Ruslana's growing settlement truly stand alone against the formidable forces to the east? Was allying with The Iron Lady a necessary compromise to ensure their survival?

These thoughts were abruptly pushed aside by a familiar shout. My heart leaped as I saw Alexis running towards me, her expression one of unguarded joy. It had been so long since I'd seen her face, not clouded by the shadow of war but open and welcoming. She threw herself into my arms, and the world seemed to narrow down to the warmth of her embrace.

Behind her, the excited barking of Lucky, her faithful companion, added to the heartfelt reunion. The joy of the moment was overwhelming, grounding me back to why I had embarked on this journey — to protect these very moments of unbridled happiness and reunion.

Days 601 and 602 were spent in whirlwind catch-ups and lengthy discussions with Ruslana and her council. I shared everything — the stark realities of The Iron Lady's rule, the barbaric advance of the Aztecos, and the potential necessity of a strategic alliance. Ruslana listened intently, her sharp mind analyzing each piece of information.

The meetings were exhaustive, stretching late into the nights. We debated strategies, potential alliances, and the hard choices that lay ahead. Ruslana was thoughtful, weighing the safety of her people against the cost of their freedom. The decision would not be easy, and it was clear she felt the weight of it deeply.

By the end of day 602, no decision had been made, but the foundations for a careful, strategic plan were being laid. Farmbridge was more than a settlement now; it was a beacon of hope for many, and whatever decision Ruslana made would ripple across the nearby lands.

As I lay down that night, the familiar sounds of Farmbridge around me, I felt a mix of exhaustion and resolve. The path forward was fraught with danger and moral quandaries, but for now, we were home. Here, in the heart of a community that had grown in the shadow of a devastated world, there was still hope for a future shaped by the choices of its people, not just the will of those who sought to rule them.

CHAPTER 4: REUNION AND RECONCILIATION

Days 603 to 605 were a blend of relief and introspection as I settled back into the life of Farmbridge, a fortress amidst chaos. The fortifications that I'd only seen in their initial stages were now complete, transforming Farmbridge into a stronghold capable of withstanding severe assaults.

Lilith and I sat on the newly erected concrete barriers, the evening sun casting long shadows over the secure expanse. "You're kind of a mess, aren't you?" she remarked, her tone a mix of humor and pointed criticism.

I smiled ruefully, unable to disagree. "I know. It's been... a lot. Leaving without explaining properly to any of you—it was the hardest choice I had to make." My voice trailed off, laden with the weight of unspoken apologies.

Lilith's expression softened. "We get why you did it, but it doesn't mean it didn't hurt," she said, her gaze shifting towards the bustling activity within the settlement. "But you're here now. That's what matters."

I nodded, grateful for her understanding yet aware of the tension my presence brought, especially with Christina and Alexis now both part of my complicated narrative.

The next few days were spent acclimatizing to the rhythms of Farmbridge. Ruslana had done more than just fortify the physical structures; she had fortified the community's spirit. Every person I met was determined, prepared to defend their home against any threat. Yet, beneath that resolve lay a palpable undercurrent of fear about the uncertainties beyond our walls— the Iron Lady's authoritarian regime and the brutal Aztecos.

Alexis and I had several long conversations, each a dance around delicate topics. She was interested in hearing about the wider world, about The Iron Lady's offers and threats. "What do you think we should do?" she asked during one of our talks, her voice steady but her eyes searching for more than just my opinion.

I took a deep breath, the weight of responsibility settling on my shoulders. "Aligning with The Iron Lady might be our only option to survive the Aztecos. She has the resources and the manpower. But it's not just about survival, Alexis—it's about how we choose to live, how we preserve our values in the face of tyranny."

Alexis nodded thoughtfully, understanding the dilemma. "And Christina?" she finally asked, her tone neutral but curious.

I paused, choosing my words carefully. "Christina... She's been a part of this journey. She knows the stakes as well as anyone."

The discussion was left open-ended, a testament to the complex web of personal and communal decisions we faced.

By day 605, I realized that Farmbridge was more than just a place of refuge; it was a testament to what could be achieved when people united under a common cause. Yet, the question remained: Could we maintain our ideals and freedom under the shadow of larger, menacing powers?

As I walked the perimeter with Lilith, reviewing our defenses, the reality of our situation was stark. "We'll make our stand here, if we have to," I said, more to myself than to her.

Lilith punched my shoulder lightly, her smirk belying the seriousness of our situation. "We always do, don't we? Just make sure you're here fighting alongside us this time."

Her words, half-teasing, half-serious, echoed in my mind as we looked out over the walls of Farmbridge. Here, amidst the burgeoning community, the battles to come seemed both distant and imminent. But for now, we were home, and we were together, and that was a victory in its own right.

Briefings and Broader Horizons

Days 606 to 610 unfolded with renewed purpose as I began to truly reintegrate into the fabric of Farmbridge under Ruslana's guidance. The place had transformed from a makeshift settlement into a burgeoning trade hub, a beacon of hope and resilience in Southern California's post-apocalyptic landscape.

Ruslana, with her characteristic blend of stern leadership and genuine pride, arranged for a series of briefings with the heads of local settlements. She was intent on forging a unified front, aware that the information I brought could reshape our collective strategies.

"As we've grown, so has our network of allies," Ruslana explained as we prepared for the first meeting. "It's time they all understand the stakes—the real threats beyond our borders."

The meeting room was filled with leaders from nearby settlements, each a testament to the growing network Ruslana had mentioned. I took the floor, detailing The Iron Lady's proposal and the chilling advance of the Aztecos. The room was tense, the air thick with concern and skepticism.

"It sounds like a dystopian nightmare," one leader commented after I described the Aztecos' brutal raids and drug-fueled warriors.

"Yes, it does," I agreed, "but it's a nightmare that's all too real and could soon be at our doorstep."

Ruslana then took over, her voice firm. "This is why we need to consider all our options. We've built something remarkable here, and I'll be damned if I let it fall without a fight."

The discussions that followed were intense and productive. We debated potential military strategies, trade routes for acquiring necessary supplies, and the possibility of deeper alliances with The Iron Lady. Each leader returned to their settlement with much to consider.

By day 610, Farmbridge was not just a sanctuary but a central hub for the region's defensive and economic planning. Ruslana's leadership had indeed transformed the area into a stronghold of both commerce and security.

However, amidst the strategic planning and meetings, personal dynamics quietly shifted. Alexis and I found moments to reconnect, navigating the complexities of our past and the undeniable tension brought about by Christina's presence.

In one quiet conversation, Alexis confessed, "I never stopped thinking about what could have been, you know. But I also can't ignore what's right in front of us."

"I know," I replied, the weight of her words settling in my chest. "There's a lot we need to figure out, both out there and in here," I added, tapping my chest.

The days concluded with a communal meeting where Ruslana addressed the entire population of Farmbridge. Her speech was inspiring, rallying the community to stand together against the looming threats.

"Together, we are more than just survivors; we are pioneers of a new world order," she proclaimed, her voice echoing through the crowd. "Let's show them what we're made of."

As the crowd dispersed, energized by Ruslana's words, I stood back, watching the faces of those I had come to care for deeply. This was more than a mission now; it was a fight for a future where fear did not hold dominion over freedom.

Days 611 to 615 promised more challenges, but for the first time in a long while, I felt we were ready to meet them head-on, as a united community with a shared vision for the future.

Days of Reflection and Preparation

Days 611 to 613 at Farmbridge were a blend of preparation and reflection as we braced for the upcoming leadership meeting. The atmosphere in the settlement buzzed with a sense of urgency and innovation. Farmbridge had become a crucible of old-world knowledge and new-world needs, with workshops dotting the landscape, churning out adapted technologies essential for survival and growth.

As I helped Ruslana's military advisors grasp the full scope of the Azteco threat, the simplicity of the tactics involved—a horrifying initial wave of human sacrifices followed by a more conventional armed assault—made the sessions more about strategizing defenses than explaining enemy tactics. Outside of these briefings, I found myself lending a hand in various capacities around the settlement, but more often than not, I found myself steering clear of Alexis, unsure how to bridge the gap that had formed between us.

Meanwhile, Watson reconnected with Alana and Clara, who had made Farmbridge their home. It was heartening to see him smile, a rare break from the stoic demeanor he'd maintained since our journey east. His interaction with them brought a semblance of normalcy, a reminder of why we fought so hard to return. However, the dark cloud of his actions, particularly the execution of the farmer's son, loomed over him—and by extension, me. The act was a necessary evil in his eyes, but it served as a stark reminder of the brutal choices we faced in the wasteland.

The gulf that had grown between Watson and me was more about the internal conflict within myself than any resentment towards him. Witnessing his decision had forced me to confront my own past decisions—actions taken in the name of survival that now haunted me in quiet moments. It wasn't just about the moral implications of those choices; it was about living with them afterward.

Days 614 to 615 were spent in further preparations for the leadership meeting. The community leaders from surrounding settlements began to arrive, each bringing news of their own challenges and the impact of our evolving trade relationships. These discussions were held in a large hall Ruslana had set aside for such purposes, a place that now served as the heart of political and strategic planning in Farmbridge.

As the leaders gathered, the hall filled with a mix of anticipation and apprehension. Ruslana opened the meeting with a strong reminder of our collective strength and the need for unity. "We stand at a crossroads," she declared, "one path leads to isolation and vulnerability, the other to strength and mutual prosperity through cooperation."

I took the floor to provide a detailed briefing on the Azteco threat, emphasizing the strategic necessity of alliance and preparedness. The response was a mix of resolve and fear— a cocktail of emotions that underscored the gravity of the situation.

As the day wound down, the leaders engaged in smaller group discussions, plotting out potential alliances and sharing intelligence that might help us predict and counter the movements of the Aztecos. The weight of leadership was visible on Ruslana's shoulders, yet she carried it with an air of determined calm.

That evening, as I walked the perimeter of Farmbridge, the fortified walls seemed both a bastion and a cage. The freedom we so cherished was shadowed by the threats outside, each day bringing us closer to potential conflict.

Reflecting on the events of the day, I realized that Farmbridge was not just a sanctuary; it was a beacon of what could be achieved when disparate groups united for a common cause. The challenge now was not just surviving, but thriving—a challenge that would test the fabric of our newfound society in the days to come.

Strategic Alignments and Diverging Paths

Days 614 to 617 unfolded under the weight of strategic planning and the unspoken fears that haunted us all. In Ruslana's operations center, a large map dominated the room, its surface a mosaic of colored pins marking our tenuous grasp on stability. Unlike The Iron Lady's command center, where strategy often veered into the realm of ruthless oppression, here it was about fostering connections and ensuring mutual survival without sacrificing our humanity.

As we gathered around the map, the tension was palpable. Ruslana, with her characteristic resolve, pointed to the markers representing our assets and allies. Green dots highlighted Farmbridge's allies to the north and south, including Big Bear, now a symbol of resilience. The infamous Slab City was marked in red, a stark reminder of the chaos that still reigned unchecked in many parts of the region.

"I won't sugarcoat it," Ruslana began, her voice firm yet infused with an underlying concern, "The Iron Lady might have the arsenal and the ruthlessness to face the Aztecos head-on, but that's not who we are. We fight for our freedom, not to replace one tyrant with another."

Alexis, standing beside me, nodded in agreement, her face shadowed by the room's dim lighting. Watson, his usual stoic self, added, "We need to fortify our defenses, yes, but more importantly, we need to strengthen our alliances. Our unity is our best weapon."

The discussion turned to the strategic positioning of our resources. The blue dots on the map represented critical supply lines and potential rally points that could serve as staging grounds for counter-assaults or refugee havens should the worst occur.

"We have to consider the possibility of needing to evacuate," I interjected, pointing to the series of blue dots that formed a corridor towards less hostile territories. "If the Aztecos push west, we'll need safe passage for our civilians."

Ruslana paused, considering this. "Good point. Let's set up contingency plans for each settlement. Evacuation routes, supply caches, emergency signals. We need a plan that covers all bases."

The meeting continued with each participant contributing their insights and suggestions. Lilith, who had been quietly observing, finally spoke up, "We also need to keep an eye on The Iron Lady. If she decides that her interests no longer align with ours, we could find ourselves facing threats from both fronts."

The meeting wrapped up with tasks assigned and a sense of cautious optimism. Despite the looming threats, there was a strong resolve to protect our way of life and support each other. We were more than just survivors; we were a community, a family forged through adversity.

As everyone started to leave, Ruslana pulled me aside. "Keep your friends close, and your enemies closer," she advised, a knowing look in her eye. "We're not just planning for an attack; we're planning to survive after it."

Walking back to my quarters, I reflected on Ruslana's words and the days ahead. The stakes were higher than ever, and the paths we choose now could very well determine the future of not just Farmbridge, but all who sought refuge under its growing influence. The challenges were immense, but so were our spirit and determination to forge a future worthy of the sacrifices so many had made.

Days 618 to 622 revolved around the critical decision regarding the National Guard Armory in the northern suburbs of Los Angeles. The urgency to secure additional resources was palpable as we grappled with the growing threats on all sides.

Ruslana, with a look of determination that matched the gravity of our situation, spearheaded the planning sessions. "We can't wait any longer," she declared in one of the meetings. "If these veterans and their community won't join us willingly, we need to prepare for other means to secure that armory."

The room was filled with leaders and military advisors, each one aware that the armory's resources could significantly bolster our defenses against both The Iron Lady's and the Aztecos' advanced threats. The atmosphere was tense, a mix of desperation and strategic calculation.

"We need a plan that minimizes conflict," I suggested. "Perhaps another delegation? This time, we stress the mutual benefits more—focus on the common threats rather than what we want from them."

Ruslana nodded thoughtfully. "I agree, but we prepare for all eventualities. If diplomacy fails, we may need to consider more direct action. It's not just about acquiring weapons; it's about ensuring the survival of everyone under our protection."

The subsequent days were a flurry of activity. Scouts were sent to gather more intelligence on the armory and its current inhabitants, while our engineers and logisticians started to prepare for a potential expedition. Simultaneously, our diplomats crafted a message that highlighted the shared dangers and the benefits of cooperation, hoping to sway the armory's residents to our cause.

As the plans solidified, I couldn't help but feel the weight of our choices. Each option came with its own set of risks and moral quandaries. The thought of potential conflict with fellow survivors was unsettling, but so was the prospect of facing well-armed enemies without sufficient resources.

On day 622, we received initial reports from our scouts. The armory was indeed as well-stocked as we hoped, but the community around it had fortified its position significantly. They were wary of outsiders, especially after numerous raids by other desperate groups.

"We'll proceed with the diplomatic mission first," Ruslana decided. "Show them that we can be allies, not threats. But we'll be ready if things take a turn."

The decision was made, and while it didn't ease the tension, it provided a clear path forward. Preparations for the diplomatic mission began in earnest, with both hope and realism guiding our steps. As we moved forward, I kept thinking about The Iron Lady's words and the eerie truth in them. Aligning with her might eventually become inevitable, but for now, we would try to forge our own path, hoping that our ideals could still prevail in a world that seemed increasingly ruled by the law of the jungle.

The Armory Mission

Days 618 to 626 were marked by a tangible tension as we journeyed north out of Farmbridge. Our contingent, bolstered by two squads from Farmbridge and an additional detachment from San Diego, made for an imposing force. As we approached Los Angeles, the reality of our mission weighed heavily on us all. The possibility of conflict loomed large, despite our hopes for a peaceful resolution.

Annie and I took turns standing guard during the nights, watching the dark silhouettes of our fellow soldiers against the dim light of our campfires. The mood was somber; everyone understood the stakes were high—not just for us, but for all the communities we represented.

"I just hope they see the reason," I murmured to Annie during one of our shifts. "This isn't just about us needing their weapons. It's about all of us surviving what's coming."

Annie nodded, her face a mask of concentration. "They will. They have to," she replied, though her voice lacked conviction.

Day 627 brought us within sight of the National Guard Armory. The community around the armory had indeed fortified its position significantly. Tall fences topped with barbed wire, watchtowers at strategic points, and patrolling guards—all spoke of a community on high alert.

We set up camp a safe distance away and prepared for the diplomatic mission. Ruslana had been clear—this was a mission of persuasion, not coercion. The following morning, I led a small delegation, including Alexis and Christina, toward the armory gates under a white flag.

The guards at the gate were initially hostile, but a combination of our sincere demeanor and the urgency of our message earned us a tentative hearing. We were escorted under close watch to a makeshift council room where we met with the armory's leaders.

I took the lead, explaining the threats looming over all our heads —the Iron Lady's ambitions and the Aztecos' brutality. "We're not here to take anything by force," I emphasized. "We're here because we believe that together, we stand a better chance against the threats outside these walls. What affects one of us eventually affects us all."

The discussions were intense and stretched over several hours. Alexis, once so reticent around me, stepped in several times to bolster our case, describing the strength that Farmbridge had developed and the mutual benefits of sharing resources and knowledge.

As the negotiations continued, I noticed Christina watching closely, her presence a silent support. The tension between us since my confession had eased slightly, replaced by a mutual understanding of the larger picture.

By day 629, we had reached an agreement. The armory's leaders, moved by our sincerity and the shared threat, agreed to a trial partnership. We would have access to some of the equipment and, in return, provide them with training and extra manpower to bolster their defenses.

It was a significant victory, one that brought a collective sigh of relief from all of us as we prepared to head back to Farmbridge. The journey back was less tense, and I could feel a shift in the dynamics of our group. There was a sense of accomplishment, a feeling that maybe, just maybe, we could face the coming storms together.

As Farmbridge's gates came into view, I felt a resolve strengthen within me. We had secured a vital alliance, and with it, a chance to fortify not just Farmbridge but all our allied communities.

The road ahead would be fraught with challenges, but for the first time in a long while, I felt hopeful about the future we were building from the ashes of the old world.

Reflections Under the Stars

Days 627 to 631 marked a period of relative peace as we traveled along the secured stretches of the Interstate 5 freeway. The collaborative efforts of the settlements had made these routes safer, a testament to the unity that was beginning to take shape among the survivor communities.

As we set camp one evening, the clearer skies revealed a brilliant tapestry of stars above us, sparking a rare moment of tranquility in the chaotic world we navigated daily. Annie and I found ourselves on watch together, seated on a small rise overlooking the camp where the flickering lights of our fire seemed to dance with the stars.

"Remember when we had to deal with that Raider's informant?" Annie asked, her voice cutting through the night's calm. I nodded, the memories vivid and unsettling.

"That was a tough night," I admitted, the weight of those actions still heavy on my conscience.

"You made a promise to me then," Annie reminded me, her gaze fixed on the starlit sky. "To keep your humanity, no matter what."

I sighed deeply, the darkness around us a stark contrast to the clarity above. "I've tried, Annie. Sometimes, I wonder if I've strayed too far."

Annie turned to look at me, her expression thoughtful. "You've kept us safe, but at a cost. It's changed you."

I nodded, my mind replaying the countless decisions and sacrifices that had marked the past two years. From securing Christina's freedom in a violent escape to the burdens of leadership in a crumbling world, each choice had left its mark.

"We're heading into a better stretch of road ahead," I changed the subject, looking forward towards the horizon where the first light of dawn promised a new day. "The settlements are working together, patrolling the highways. It's something, right?"

Annie smiled slightly, "It's a start. But don't lose sight of who you are in the grand scheme of things. The world's rough, but we need to hold onto what makes us human."

Her words resonated with me as we watched the rest of the night unfold. The stars, a constant reminder of the world's vastness and beauty, seemed to echo her sentiments.

As dawn approached, our conversation drifted to lighter topics, the burdens of the past momentarily lifted by the promise of a new day. We talked about the future, about what Farmbridge could become with its new allies and the challenges that still lay ahead.

By the time we returned to camp to wake the others, I felt a renewed sense of purpose. Yes, the world had changed, and yes, we had been forced to adapt in ways we never imagined. But as long as there were people like Annie reminding me of the importance of our humanity, there was hope.

Hope that we could rebuild something worthwhile, hope that despite the darkness, the stars would always return to remind us of the light.

Days 632 to 636 were tense as we waited for the final squad to arrive. The delay was due to a skirmish with raiders, a stark reminder of the volatile world we inhabited. It underscored the urgency of our mission—not just to secure resources but to maintain the fragile safety we had managed to carve out amidst the chaos.

As we set camp outside the ruins of Los Angeles, the leaders of each settlement convened around a hastily set up table, illuminated by the harsh glow of lanterns against the encroaching darkness. The air was thick with the potential of conflict, both external and internal.

Ruslana stood firm, her voice steady as she outlined the stakes. "Access to the Armory is crucial. It's not just about weapons—it's about securing our future. If we need to fight, we will."

I could see Alexis's discomfort with the direction of the conversation. Her ideals clashed visibly with the harsh realities presented by Ruslana. Despite this, there was a palpable understanding among the group that idealism had to be tempered with the practical needs of survival.

The plan was to approach the Armory with a combined force of diplomacy and readiness to use force if necessary. "We'll try talking first," I suggested, hoping to bridge the gap between the two stances. "Let's show them we're serious about cooperation, not conquest. Maybe they'll see the benefit of joining us."

This approach was met with mixed reactions. Some nodded in

agreement, appreciating the attempt to balance morality with necessity, while others remained skeptical, their faces hardened by too many betrayals and losses.

The final day before the squad arrived was spent in rigorous preparation. We drilled, checked equipment, and reviewed every possible scenario—from peaceful negotiations to a full-scale assault. Alexis spent time training some of the younger volunteers, her way of coping with the moral complexities by focusing on preparation and protection.

When the squad finally arrived, they brought with them not just the scars of their recent battle but also vital intelligence —they had intercepted communications indicating that the community around the Armory was equally anxious about potential attacks from larger forces like The Iron Lady's.

This information shifted the dynamic of our planning. "They're scared, just like us," I pointed out during the briefing that evening. "Maybe they're more ready to talk than we think."

With this new understanding, we adjusted our approach. It was decided that a smaller, unarmed delegation would approach the Armory first, offering medical supplies and food as a gesture of goodwill. I volunteered to lead this group, hoping that a show of vulnerability might pave the way for trust.

Days 637 to 641 would be critical. As we broke camp the next morning, the weight of our mission was palpable. But there was also a cautious thread of hope—we were armed not just with weapons, but with a plan that might allow us to uphold our ideals without sacrificing our security. The challenge would be to maintain this delicate balance long enough to make a difference.

Lady for a fall while ensuring Farm Bridge could rise above the chaos and violence. This was a complex and dangerous strategy, but Christina's insights shed light on a possible path forward that could balance morality with the harsh necessities of survival.

"We could work on strengthening Farm Bridge's alliances," I suggested, thinking aloud. "Make them strong enough to defend themselves without resorting to the Iron Lady's methods."

Christina turned to face me, her silhouette faintly outlined by the moonlight filtering through the tent fabric. "And what about the Iron Lady? Just leave her to deal with the Aztecos on her own?"

I paused, considering the weight of that decision. "Maybe not entirely on her own. We could set conditions, help her fight the Aztecos but ensure she doesn't overrun everything we've built here. We push for reforms, maybe."

"It's a fine line," Christina murmured. "Playing both sides so they don't play us."

I nodded slowly. "It's going to require a lot of diplomacy, and probably more fighting. But if we can navigate this right, maybe we can avoid becoming what we're fighting against."

Christina laid her hand on mine, her grip firm. "Just remember, whatever you choose, make sure it's something you can live with. You've seen enough to know the costs of these choices."

Her words echoed in my head as I lay awake long into the night, the laughter outside fading into the occasional crackle of the campfire. The path ahead was fraught with moral ambiguities and the potential for great cost, but also the possibility of a future where the ideals of Farm Bridge could form the blueprint for a new civilization, one that could rise from the ashes of the old without mirroring its darkest aspects.

The leader, a grizzled veteran named Carson, listened intently to Ruslana's pitch. He glanced around at our assembled force, his eyes lingering on the various armaments and soldiers before returning his focus to Ruslana.

"We've been holding out here since the collapse, keeping these weapons safe from raiders and slavers," Carson said, his voice gruff with the weight of responsibility. "Why should we share them with you? How do I know you won't turn them on us later?"

Ruslana's response was firm yet diplomatic. "Because we're not raiders or slavers. We're building something different, and we need all the help we can get. The Aztecos don't care about our squabbles. If they come through here, they won't differentiate between your people and ours."

I could see Carson considering her words, the lines of his face deepening with thought. After a long pause, he finally nodded. "Let me talk it over with my council. I can't make this decision alone."

Ruslana agreed, and the meeting ended with a tentative sense of hope. As they departed, I caught Ruslana's eye, and she gave me a small nod. It was a risky play, inviting them to see our strength and vulnerabilities, but it was necessary. It highlighted the reality that in the face of a common enemy, old grievances needed to be set aside.

Over the next few days, as we awaited their decision, the tension at camp was palpable. Everyone understood the stakes were high. This armory could mean the difference between survival and annihilation. The waiting was the hardest part, each hour stretching out with excruciating slowness as we contemplated the future of our nascent alliance.

If we don't stand together, no amount of ammunition or guns will save any of us. We're not just asking for weapons; we're asking you to join us."

Johnson looked at Alexis for a long moment, then around at all of us. His gaze lingered on the armed men and women from both groups, the tension palpable in the air. Finally, he let out a long sigh.

"I'll discuss this with my council. It's not just my call. These weapons aren't just material; they're our leverage, our safety net." He paused, then added, "But you make a compelling case. Give us some time to think it over. We'll give you our answer tomorrow."

As Johnson and his team retreated back to their fortified compound, the atmosphere among us shifted slightly, from one of confrontation to cautious optimism. Alexis's words had clearly made an impact, highlighting the shared vulnerability and the real stakes if we failed to unite.

That night, back at our camp, Ruslana convened a quick meeting with all of us. "Alexis, that was... unexpected. Effective but unexpected," she admitted with a grudging respect. The others murmured their agreement, impressed with Alexis's ability to articulate the fears and hopes that all of us were feeling but struggled to express.

We spent a restless night, each of us lost in our thoughts about the future. The unity Alexis spoke of was our best hope, but it hinged on the Armory's decision. Would they see the wisdom in standing together, or would they choose isolation, focusing only on the immediate safety of their walls? The answer would determine much about the future of all our settlements.

Negotiations at the Armory

The group was diverse, representing a range of experiences from former military personnel to community leaders who had taken on leadership roles post-disaster. We stayed in a designated area for visitors, giving us a sense of their hospitality but also their caution. Over the next few days, we held discussions that were intense but necessary.

Ruslana led most of the talks, with Alexis occasionally chiming in. The tension from the initial confrontation had lessened somewhat, and the leaders were now more willing to listen. They asked detailed questions about the threats we described— the Iron Lady's army and the Aztecos. We shared everything we knew: numbers, tactics, and the sheer brutality of their attacks.

Johnson, who had seemed so resistant at first, was particularly interested in the strategic implications. "If they've beaten an army as well-prepared as you say the Iron Lady's is, what chance do we have isolated like this?" he pondered aloud during one of the sessions.

It was a question that hung heavily in the room, and Ruslana took it as her cue to outline a proposal for a mutual defense pact. "We don't just need your weapons," she reiterated, "we need your people, your skills. We need to stand together, or else we all fall separately."

The meetings continued, stretching late into the night, each session ending with a sense that progress was being made, albeit slowly. The leaders from the Armory were cautious, understandably weighing the potential risk against the urgent need Ruslana and our group presented.

By the fourth day, the atmosphere had shifted significantly. The Armory's leaders had started to see us less as potential raiders and more as desperate allies facing a common threat. The change was subtle but undeniable in the way they engaged with our proposals and shared their own concerns and strategic ideas.

We waited anxiously as they convened privately to make their final decision, hoping that the unity we had argued for so passionately would finally come to fruition.

Reconnaissance Mission to the South

The agreement was struck with a nervous tension hanging in the air. Johnson selected one of his most trusted men, a seasoned ex-military like myself, named Marcus. In return, Alexis stayed behind as a gesture of good faith. I couldn't help but feel the weight of her safety on my shoulders as we prepared to leave.

Our goal was clear: to head south and gather undeniable proof of the Azteco threat. If Marcus could see firsthand the kind of danger lurking beyond the borders, he could be the voice we needed to persuade the Armory's leaders. The journey south was planned meticulously; we would avoid major roads to prevent attracting attention, moving through less traveled paths that I had learned about during my time with the Iron Lady.

As we set out, the atmosphere among our small team was one of cautious optimism. Marcus, though obviously wary, was open-minded. "I'm here to see the truth," he stated plainly as we loaded up the last of our supplies. His professionalism was reassuring, and I found myself hoping not just for the success of our mission, but also for his safe return, knowing the stakes involved for Alexis and myself.

The first leg of our journey was uneventful, but the tension never eased. Each rustle in the underbrush, every distant noise made us grip our weapons tighter. We made camp as the sun set, taking turns on watch. That night, under the clear skies finally free of debris, the stars seemed to watch over us, silent witnesses to the unfolding drama below.

By the time we reached the southern outpost on the second day, the reality of our mission had set in. We approached cautiously, using binoculars to scout ahead. The camp was indeed there, just as the intelligence reports had described, teeming with Azteco activity. The sight of their guards, unmistakable with their fearsome decorations and weaponry, was chilling.

We documented everything from a distance—taking photos, noting numbers, observing their routines. The evidence was damning, and Marcus watched, his face hardening with each passing hour. "I had no idea," he murmured at one point, his voice almost lost in the wind.

Our return journey was heavy with the burden of what we had witnessed. Marcus was quiet, deep in thought, and I wondered what his report would say once we got back. Would it be enough to sway the Armory's leaders? Or would it only harden their resolve to defend their own, leaving Farmbridge and its allies to fend for themselves?

As the outlines of the Armory appeared on the horizon, a mix of relief and apprehension filled me. We had completed our mission, but the hardest part was yet to come.

Preparation and Departure

The preparation for our mission took meticulous planning. Watson, understanding his emotional ties with Alana, stayed behind at my insistence, his usual stoic demeanor giving way to a brief show of reluctance. Annie, on the other hand, insisted on coming along, her determination clear and unyielding. Lilith wanted to join too but eventually agreed to remain with Alexis, ensuring she wasn't left alone amidst strangers.

Claiborne, the representative from the Armory's settlement, turned out to be a seasoned veteran like myself. His easy-going nature was a relief; having someone difficult could have complicated the mission further. We spent a day discussing tactics, routes, and what we hoped to achieve. Claiborne's military experience was evident, and his input proved invaluable as we refined our plan.

Ruslana took on the task of coordinating our passage south discreetly. She needed to adjust patrol routes temporarily to ensure our movement remained unnoticed by potential informants. This required careful manipulation of patrol schedules and routes—a complex task, but essential for maintaining the secrecy of our operation.

Once everything was in place, we gathered our gear and prepared to depart. Christina decided to return to Farmbridge with Ruslana's group, which was a hard goodbye. I assured her of my return, but the uncertainty of the mission lay heavily between us. With final checks and a deep breath, our small team was ready to head out, leaving behind the relative safety of the Armory for the uncertainties that awaited us in the southern territories.

The first leg of our journey was uneventful, marked by silent treks through less-traveled paths and nights spent under the stars, discussing softly the possible outcomes of our mission. The weight of responsibility was palpable, each of us aware of the stakes involved—not just for ourselves, but for all the communities back north. As we moved closer to our destination, the reality of what we might find—and the decisions we might have to make—grew ever more pressing.

The journey south was fraught with caution and quiet intensity. We avoided the main roads, weaving through lesser-known trails and often doubling back to ensure no one was trailing us. The threat of the Aztecos loomed large—not just their brutality but their cunning in espionage that The Iron Lady had warned about. Their spies, often disguised as captives or seemingly harmless wanderers, could have been anywhere.

Our path took us through areas that were once bustling with life but now lay in desolation. The ruins of cities, now havens for raiders and desperate survivors, presented a new set of challenges. Each pile of rubble could have been a potential ambush point, each hollowed-out building a sniper's nest. We moved cautiously, often pausing to scout ahead before proceeding.

Claiborne, familiar with military tactics yet unfamiliar with this new, ruthless enemy, adapted quickly. His input was crucial, his eyes often catching details that others missed. Annie, ever vigilant, covered our rear, her rifle never far from her hands.

The silence of the destroyed cities was unnerving. The lack of human noise, save for our own careful movements, was a stark reminder of the catastrophe that had befallen humanity. Yet, it was in these quiet moments that the gravity of our mission sank in deeper. We weren't just fighting for survival; we were fighting to preserve what little humanity was left.

Every night, under the scant cover of ruins or the sparse desert brush, we camped in shifts. Sleep was light and often interrupted by the slightest noise—a distant crash, the wind picking up, or the occasional distant shout that reminded us of the dangers lurking all around.

As we neared the southern border, the landscape began to change. The ruins gave way to more open desert, and the real test of our resolve began. It was here that we would find out if our preparations were enough, if our caution had been warranted, and ultimately, if we could face what lay ahead not just as soldiers or survivors, but as defenders of a future we still hoped could exist.

Navigating Challenges and Reflecting on Leadership

As we made our way to the outskirts of San Diego, I got to know Clay better. He shared stories from before everything changed. He and his girlfriend had enjoyed a seemingly idyllic life by the ocean, and post-military, he'd dabbled in digital media with an online show. Surprisingly, both had survived the initial chaos of the world ending, eventually finding refuge with the Armory group. His easygoing nature made him an invaluable part of our journey, and his relationship survived the odds, a rare beacon of hope in these times.

During our travels, the conversation often turned to the delicate balance of leadership and ethics in this new world. Alexis's debates with Ruslana back at the Armory echoed in my mind.

Ruslana's stance was eerily reminiscent of The Iron Lady's—both were prepared to secure necessary resources by any means. Yet, Alexis's counterpoint was poignant: the sustainability of power seized through force was dubious at best.

This internal conflict was a constant companion as we navigated the treacherous ruins. Every step kicked up dust laced with low levels of radiation—a silent, pervasive threat. We covered our faces, traveled by night to avoid the heat and exposure, and rested by day in whatever shelter we could find.

Reflecting on these leadership styles, I found myself grappling with the complexities of survival versus morality. The Iron Lady's method—ruthless efficiency aimed at the greater good— was effective but brutal. Ruslana seemed to be veering toward a similar path under the pressure of impending threats.

However, Alexis's words lingered: "How long do you expect to hold on to that which you take by force?" This question became a central theme of our discussions as we prepared for the potential conflicts ahead. It wasn't just about surviving the present; it was about building a future that wouldn't perpetuate the cycle of violence and retribution that seemed to define so much of our current world.

As we approached the outskirts of San Diego, these thoughts weighed heavily. Our mission was clear, but the ethical implications were complex. How we chose to handle the next few days could define not just our survival, but the kind of legacy we would leave in this new and uncertain world.

Venturing into Azteco Territory

As we ventured deeper into the wild lands leading to the Mexican border, the reminders of civilization dwindled further.

Ruslana's last allied settlement lay a day's journey behind us, marking the edge of known and somewhat controlled territories. Beyond this point, the landscape was dominated by remnants of chaotic upheavals, areas where no group had successfully forged relations post-collapse.

The narratives from refugees painted a grim picture of Mexico post-disaster. Government structures had crumbled overnight, leaving a power vacuum swiftly filled by drug cartels. These groups, previously armed for the narcotics trade, found themselves inadvertently prepped for a dystopian survival scenario. Yet, this readiness spiraled into a vicious conflict over scarce resources and clean land, culminating in a brutal war among the cartels themselves. From this strife, the Aztecos emerged dominant, a group known for their ruthless consolidation of power and territorial aggression.

Our destination lay southward towards the Gulf of California, planning to cross into Sonora where the western fringes of Azteco territory began. Near the town of Caborca, there was rumored to be a significant Azteco settlement—a pivotal location for demonstrating to Clay the grave threat looming over us all.

To minimize detection, we chose a path well away from main roads and urban ruins, aiming to skirt around potential hotspots of activity. This route was meant to keep us hidden from the eyes of hostile groups, a necessity in regions where the law of the land was dictated by firepower and cruelty.

Days 675 to 677 brought an unexpected challenge. It wasn't the sight but the sound of danger that alerted us—horses. The rhythmic beating of hooves against the arid ground reached us before we could see their riders. Tension gripped our small group as we prepared for a potential encounter, knowing full well that any meeting here could swiftly turn lethal. We braced, ready to face whatever emerged from the dusty horizon.

Infiltrating Azteco Territory

As we continued deeper into unfamiliar territory, the political landscape was as unknown as the geographical one. Without knowledge of who had survived and where allegiances lay, our journey southward was marked by extreme caution, which inevitably slowed our progress.

Our objective was clear: infiltrate the Azteco settlement undetected and provide Clay with undeniable proof of the imminent threat. We decided on a risky but potentially effective disguise: we would pose as slavers, with Annie reluctantly agreeing to act as our captive. This role, while distasteful, leveraged the unfortunate reality that a young woman would likely not arouse suspicion in such a lawless area.

We adjusted Annie's appearance to fit the part, ensuring she looked the part of a detainee without compromising her safety or dignity. We were all too aware of the potential dangers this plan posed, but the urgent need to convey the severity of the Azteco menace to Clay overshadowed our reservations.

Traveling by night to avoid the scorching daytime heat and the eyes of any watchful enemies, we kept to the shadows and less traveled paths. Each member of our small team was acutely aware of the stakes involved, not just for ourselves but for the communities we hoped to protect.

As we neared the outskirts of the suspected Azteco territory, tension among us grew. Every step forward was weighed with the potential of discovery, and the knowledge that we were walking into the heart of darkness, possibly surrounded by enemies who thrived on cruelty and chaos.

Encounters on the Gulf of California Coast

Upon reaching a quaint coastal village along the Gulf of California, we spent a full day observing from a safe distance. It was crucial to determine the residents' affiliations—if any—and their general demeanor. The villagers appeared to lead simple lives, relying heavily on fishing and small-scale agriculture, seemingly untouched by the chaos that had swallowed much of the world.

Despite the potential risks of nuclear fallout affecting marine life and the subsequent acidification of the ocean, these families seemed to have adapted to their new reality. Their daily routines revolved around the sea and the land, suggesting a resilience that was both admirable and poignant given the broader global context.

Feeling reasonably confident about their neutrality, we decided to approach them. Our interaction was cautious but friendly, aiming to establish trust and secure essential resources for our journey. In exchange for their hospitality and the use of a boat, we offered them valuable medical supplies, including first aid kits, which they accepted with evident gratitude.

Their warm reception was a stark contrast to the war-torn regions we'd left behind. It was a reminder of the pockets of humanity that persisted in even the most isolated or overlooked places. This brief encounter provided not just practical assistance but a momentary respite from the constant tension of our mission, reminding us of the ordinary lives that continued in the shadow of global upheaval.

Tense Moments in the Coastal Village

On our final day in the coastal village, as we were preparing to depart, an urgent alarm was raised. Dust trails signaled the rapid approach of horsemen, and a sense of dread settled over the villagers. An elderly woman quickly ushered us into a nearby house, advising us to remain silent and hidden.

Despite her warnings, we readied our rifles, anticipating trouble. Four men arrived shortly after, exuding arrogance and authority. They dismounted and began to harass the villagers, demanding tribute. It became painfully evident that these men were here to enforce their will through intimidation and violence.

The villagers, in an attempt to appease these bullies, hastily gathered what little they could—fish and crops, the fruits of their hard labor. However, their offerings were met with scorn. The leader's anger flared when he deemed the tribute insufficient. Without hesitation, he seized a young woman, intending to take her as payment. His accomplice followed suit, grabbing another girl.

The scene was chillingly familiar, echoing the injustices I had witnessed and fought against throughout these troubled times. The parallels to Christina's past enslavement and the potential dangers Alexis had faced were stark in my mind.

Compelled by a mix of rage and a deep-seated need to protect those who couldn't defend themselves, I stepped out from our hiding place. Without waiting for Annie or Clay to catch up or even fully assessing the risk, I confronted the thugs. My voice rang out clear and authoritative, demanding they release the young women immediately.

A Harrowing Arrival in Azteco Territory

After a long and tense day of crossing the Gulf of California, we finally made landfall on the opposite shore. The boat we used was modest, powered by a minimal engine that, at times, seemed barely capable of keeping us afloat. However, fortune was on our side, and we managed to reach the other side without incident.

We discovered a secluded cove that offered an ideal hiding spot for our boat. With concerted effort, we hauled it up the sandy beach and secured it to a large boulder, ensuring it would remain undisturbed.

The reality of our mission weighed heavily on us as we stood on the foreign sand, knowing we were deep within Azteco territory. This was the heartland of the brutal force we had come to investigate. The air was thick with the salty tang of the sea, mingled with a sense of impending danger.

Now, far from any familiar faces or friendly outposts, we had to rely solely on our wits and each other. The isolation was palpable, pressing in from the silent expanse around us. Our next steps would take us deeper into hostile lands, where every shadow could conceal a threat.

As we gathered our gear and prepared to move inland, I couldn't shake the image of the villagers' distraught faces. Their words echoed in my mind, a grim reminder of the complex moral landscape we navigated. It was a stark lesson in the unintended consequences that often follow even well-intentioned actions.

We made our way deeper into Azteco territory, our appearances altered drastically to blend in. Annie carried only a sidearm, hidden from view, while Clay and I adorned ourselves with the typical Azteco warrior makeup, using bright and chaotic patterns to mimic their fearsome appearance. Despite our concerns, our American identities didn't seem to cause suspicion; the Aztecos were not discriminatory in their recruitment or brutality.

As we traveled, the eerie silence from the local traders was unsettling. Their downcast eyes and swift avoidance spoke volumes of the fear that governed this land. The further we ventured, the more the stark reality of the Aztecos' reign of terror became evident. We encountered bodies displayed grotesquely along the roadsides—each a macabre trophy of torture and execution, often marked with crudely painted or carved 'crimes' on their skin or nearby surfaces.

The chilling sights were relentless and served to convince Clay of the dire narratives I had shared about the Aztecos. Each gruesome scene underscored the monstrous nature of this group and their brutal enforcement of control.

By day 697, we approached a large settlement that seemed to serve as a central hub for the Aztecos. The size and structure of the community suggested it was more than just a temporary encampment; it was a stronghold, fortified and bustling with activity. The air was thick with tension, the streets busy with people who carried the same mix of fear and resignation we'd seen earlier.

We prepared ourselves for what was to come, knowing that our mission was about to reach its most critical phase. We needed to gather as much intelligence as possible without drawing attention to our true purpose. As we moved through the settlement, every interaction, every observation was crucial. We were in the heart of enemy territory, and every moment counted.

Infiltrating Kaborka

Upon entering Kaborka, we stepped into a setting that seemed ripped from the pages of history, reconstructed into a living homage to ancient Aztec culture. The Aztecos had not merely settled here; they had transformed the town, demolishing much of the modern structures to erect replicas of ancient pyramids and temples using forced labor.

The transformation was shockingly extensive, with several smaller pyramids scattered about and a colossal one dominating the skyline. The attention to detail in mimicking ancient architecture was unnerving, showcasing the group's commitment to their identity, but it was a commitment forged through cruelty and domination.

The streets of Kaborka were bustling, teeming with people that provided us the cover we needed to remain inconspicuous. This had evolved far beyond a simple border outpost as previously reported by The Iron Lady's spies. Its expansion was a clear and present danger to surrounding areas, including potentially Farmbridge and Arizona. The speed of this expansion suggested that within a year, they could reach further into U.S. territory.

To secure accommodation, we traded ammunition and grenades. Medical supplies held little value here, underscoring the brutal nature of life under Azteco rule. We maintained the ruse of Annie being our captive, which, while distasteful, granted us the necessary facade to navigate through the town without drawing undue attention.

The Aztecos had revived not only the architectural styles of their namesake but also their darkest rituals. Human sacrifice was a prevalent and celebrated event, woven into the fabric of daily life. The central pyramid served as a gruesome altar where life was routinely extinguished in public ceremonies.

The existence of a thriving slave market was among the most harrowing sights. The market was a hub of despair, where human beings were traded like commodities. Some of these slaves met their end on the sacrificial pyramids, a fact that visibly shook Clay to his core.

Seeing firsthand the horrors of Azteco society was overwhelming. Clay's resolve hardened as the reality of what these people endured under Azteco rule became undeniably clear. It was evident that without significant intervention, the spread of this terror would continue unabated, posing a severe threat to all neighboring regions.

As I ventured alone through the streets of Kaborka, seeking more detailed intelligence about the Aztecos' expansion plans, I traded ammunition and homemade liquor for information. The Aztecos were not just holding ceremonies; they were actively expanding their control north and west, overwhelming the few remaining drug cartels. These cartels were on the brink of annihilation, soon to be another set of victims sacrificed to the Azteco gods.

However, I had let my guard down. Absorbed in my task, I failed to notice an approaching figure until his arm was choking me from behind. Instinctively, I bit down hard on his arm, earning a yell of pain. Using the momentary shock to my advantage, I elbowed him in the stomach. But before I could free myself, a second man struck me on the head with a club, and I crumpled to the ground, dazed and disoriented.

As I struggled to regain my senses, the second man wiped the paint from my face, exposing my true identity. "Good, gringo," he sneered, recognizing that I was an outsider. "You have a lot of fights. You'll do well for me in the arena."

His words sent a chill through me as I realized the gravity of my situation. I was now a captive, likely to be thrown into some brutal spectacle to entertain the Aztecos. The mission to gather intelligence had taken a dangerous turn, and my immediate concern was survival and escape.

CHAPTER 5:
THE ARENA

Awakening to another splash of icy water, my senses gradually pieced together my grim reality. I was still held captive by the Aztecos, and my forced ingestion of hallucinogens continued, distorting my perception and weakening my resolve. Yet, the cold water served as a harsh reminder that I was alive and had a forthcoming challenge to face.

Rough hands hauled me from my cage early that morning and dragged me to what I could only assume was an arena. The sun was just cresting the horizon, casting long shadows and bathing the area in a soft, ominous light. The arena was a crude circle defined by large stones and sand, surrounded by raucous spectators who clamored for violence and spectacle.

As I stood there, swaying slightly from the drugs still coursing through my system, a gate opposite me creaked open. My heart raced as a figure emerged—a man almost as battered as I, his eyes hollow with despair yet burning with a desperate will to survive. It was clear he was no stranger to this horrifying ritual.

The crowd's cheers crescendoed, hungry for the brutality about to unfold. The overseer of this macabre event—a towering man adorned with Aztec-inspired tattoos and a grim expression— gave the signal to begin.

Despite the fog in my brain, survival instincts kicked in. As the man charged, I sidestepped, using his momentum to throw him off balance. We exchanged blows, each punch fueled by the primal need to survive rather than any malice. The fight was brutal and exhausting, dragging on under the sun's unforgiving glare.

As our battle reached its weary end, I managed to pin him down, my hands poised to deliver a final, fatal strike. Our eyes met, and in that brief moment, I saw not an enemy but a fellow victim of circumstance, caught in a struggle neither of us wanted.

I hesitated—a moment of mercy or perhaps weakness, I couldn't tell which. The crowd's bloodlust turned to anger at the lack of a deathly finale. Before the overseer could decide my fate for sparing the man, a commotion at the edge of the arena caught everyone's attention.

Annie, Clay, and a group of unexpected allies had infiltrated the gathering, creating a distraction that sparked chaos among the spectators. Seizing the moment, I grabbed the downed man, pulling him with me as we escaped through the chaos towards the freedom that beckoned just beyond the confines of the Azteco nightmare.

As we fled, the reality of our situation set in—we were not just escaping an arena; we were running from a way of life that thrived on the suffering of others. The path ahead was fraught with danger, but for the first time in days, hope glimmered on the horizon.

Trial by Fire

After the searing rush of the powder, I found myself locked

alone in a dimly lit stone chamber, the door clanging shut with ominous finality. The room was bare, with walls that echoed back the faint sounds of the arena outside—cheers mixed with cries of anguish. The air was thick, heavy with the scent of dust and old blood.

As the drug-induced haze began to warp my perceptions, shadows in the corners of the room seemed to move, coalescing into forms both menacing and ephemeral. I shook my head, trying to clear the fog, but the drug was potent, designed to heighten aggression and dull fear. My heart pounded fiercely, and my hands clenched involuntarily.

Minutes—or was it hours?—passed in tense anticipation. Then, suddenly, the far wall of the room began to slide open with a grinding noise, revealing a pathway illuminated by flickering torchlight. Hesitant yet compelled, I stepped forward, the echoes of my footsteps bouncing off the narrow stone walls leading me deeper into a labyrinthine network beneath the arena.

The passage twisted and turned, each corner presenting a new horror. In one alcove, grotesque carvings depicted scenes of battle and sacrifice, the figures almost seeming to move in the dancing torchlight. In another, bones were piled carelessly, the remnants of previous contenders who had fallen victim to this cruel trial.

Eventually, the corridor opened into a larger chamber where the true test awaited. Two other figures were already there, as disoriented and tense as I, their eyes wild with the same forced fury. The room was an arena in miniature, surrounded by steep walls too high to climb, with weapons scattered haphazardly across the ground.

A voice boomed from above, reverberating off the stone. "Prove your worth, or join the ancestors in defeat!" It was clear—fight or die. The other two lunged for weapons, a rusted machete and a broken spear. I followed suit, my hand closing around the cold grip of a short sword.

The clash was inevitable. We circled, eyes locked, each of us battling not just for survival but against the drugs coursing through our veins, urging us toward savagery. The first exchange was swift and brutal, the clang of metal on metal ringing in my ears. I parried a wild swing, countering with a thrust that grazed my opponent's side. He stumbled back, pain momentarily clearing the madness from his eyes.

The fight was desperate, driven by the primal need to survive, but also marred by the understanding that we were pawns in a macabre game. With each movement, I felt the pull of the drug, a fierce joy in the combat that was both exhilarating and horrifying.

As the battle raged, a plan formed in my mind. If I could just hold out, if I could just keep my wits about me, there might be a chance not just to survive, but to turn this trial on its captors. With a fierce cry, I rallied, channeling all my strength into a decisive blow that would end the fight—but not the war. I was determined to break free from this cycle of violence, to escape this hellish arena and return to those who believed in a future worth fighting for, a future far from the dark depths of the aztecos' bloody sport.

The Arena Battle

In the dazzling light of the arena, my senses were overwhelmed by the deafening cheers from the crowd. My opponent, the Azteco warrior, stood confidently across the sandy ground, his body adorned with the vivid markings of a jaguar, his eyes sizing me up as a worthy foe. The obsidian blade he wielded gleamed menacingly in the sun, promising a swift and brutal confrontation.

Driven by the relentless effects of the drug coursing through my veins, I charged at him with a primal ferocity that I barely recognized in myself. Every fiber of my being was focused on survival, on the fight before me. The Azteco warrior met my charge with a disciplined calm, a stark contrast to my reckless aggression.

As I closed the distance, the warrior shifted his stance, his body poised to strike with precision. He swung his blade in a wide arc, aiming to catch me off-guard. But the drug had heightened my reflexes unnaturally. I ducked under the swing, feeling the whoosh of the blade just inches above my head.

Using my momentum, I tackled him at the waist, hoping to use my weight to bring him down. The crowd roared louder, feeding off the intensity of our struggle. The warrior stumbled but regained his balance, pushing me back with a strength that matched his skill.

We circled each other, each assessing the other's next move. I noticed the sandy floor of the arena, thinking quickly to use it to my advantage. Kicking up a cloud of sand, I aimed to distract him, to blind him momentarily. He shielded his face with his arm, and in that split second of obscured vision, I lunged.

However, the warrior was seasoned, anticipating my tactics. He sidestepped, and his counterattack was swift—a sharp thrust aimed at my side. I felt the searing pain as the obsidian blade sliced through my shirt, grazing my skin. Adrenaline surged, and I ignored the pain, grabbing his wrist and twisting it hard.

The blade dropped from his grasp, and for a moment, we grappled fiercely, strength against strength. My heart pounded in my ears, the crowd's cheers a distant echo. I managed to wrestle him to the ground, pinning him beneath me. My hands found his throat, and for a moment, I hesitated—this was not me; this was the drug.

But survival took over. I tightened my grip, ready to end it, when suddenly, a sharp pain exploded in my side. The warrior had managed to retrieve a small dagger from his belt, driving it into my flesh. The pain was sharp, real, snapping me back to a harsh reality.

Rolling away, I clutched at my side, blood warm between my fingers. The warrior stood, breathing heavily, his eyes acknowledging the challenge I posed. As we both prepared to continue, the crowd's anticipation was palpable, eager for more of the brutal spectacle we provided.

This fight was far from over, but in that moment, I understood the depths of what I had become part of—a barbaric display of survival at its most primal. Yet, there was no turning back. I stood up, ready to face whatever came next, determined to survive, to return to those who still believed in a world beyond this savagery.

Aftermath and Reflection

After my violent victory in the arena, I was relocated to a larger, more secluded cage, a step up from the squalid confines I had previously occupied. This new space offered not just physical comfort but also a momentary mental respite, allowing me to process the tumultuous events.

The effect of the Fuego, the drug that had supercharged my aggression and strength, slowly ebbed away, leaving a heavy fatigue in its wake. As the drug's influence diminished, so did the red haze that had clouded my vision and judgment during the fight. The clarity that returned was painful, filled with the stark reality of what I had done.

Despite the comfort of the new cage, I felt trapped in more ways than one. The physical bars were obvious, but the psychological chains were heavier. The crowd's reaction to the fight—half cheering, half calling for blood—echoed in my mind, a disturbing reminder of the primal entertainment I had provided.

I spent those days largely in isolation, grappling with the dual nature of my actions. On one hand, I had survived; on the other, I had succumbed to the very barbarism I despised. The quiet in the cage was punctuated only by the occasional visits from guards bringing food and water, each encounter a silent exchange that underscored my captivity.

In the solitude of my cage, I reflected on the broader implications of my actions. The drug, the fight, and the crowd's reaction were all pieces of a larger puzzle that depicted a society reveling in violence and spectacle. This was the world of the Aztecos, a society built on the glorification of brutality.

My thoughts frequently turned to my friends and the mission that had brought me here. The need to expose the reality of the Azteco threat was more pressing than ever. I knew that escaping this place and bringing back critical information was essential, not just for my survival but for the survival of all the settlements that stood on the brink of confrontation with this ruthless enemy.

The days passed slowly, each hour stretching as I battled the despair that threatened to take hold. But even in the darkest moments, a resolve grew within me—a resolve to not only escape this hellish place but to fight against the darkness it represented. I knew that the journey ahead would be fraught with danger, but the stakes were too high to ignore.

By the end of the third day, as the last traces of the Fuego left my system, I felt a renewed sense of purpose. My mind was clearer, my determination firmer. I was ready to plan my escape, to return to my friends with invaluable insights and to confront the looming threat of the Aztecos head-on. The fight in the arena had ended, but the battle for the future was just beginning.

Survival in the Arena

I continued to fight in the arena, each battle a blur of rage fueled by the drug known as Fuego. The white powder that had first disoriented me was administered less frequently now, but the red drug was given to me right before each fight, igniting a fiery aggression within me. This concoction transformed me into a relentless warrior, capable of confronting my opponents with a ferocious intensity that was both exhilarating and terrifying.

The effects of the Fuego were profound. It not only enhanced my physical capabilities but also diminished my fear, making me an ideal participant in the brutal spectacles that entertained the crowds. The drug induced a state where pain and fear were distant echoes, allowing me to perform feats of violence that drew cheers and gasps from the onlookers.

After each fight, as the drug's influence waned, I would return to my cage, each time discovering new injuries on my body. These wounds were treated cursorily if at all, serving as stark reminders of the battles I had endured. Despite the pain, survival was a potent motivator, and the promise of better treatment for continued success in the arena provided a grim kind of incentive to keep fighting.

The man in the white suit, whom I had come to recognize as the orchestrator of these gruesome events, seemed pleased with my performance. His visits became more frequent, each time reinforcing the harsh reality of my situation: fight well, and I would be granted the basic necessities that made life in captivity bearable. This transactional existence was dehumanizing, yet it was the currency of survival in this twisted society.

As days turned into weeks, the routine became agonizingly familiar. I was trapped in a cycle of combat, recovery, and brief periods of respite, punctuated by the administration of drugs that prepared me for the next fight. The clarity between these bouts was filled with a deepening sense of despair and a burning desire for escape, but the opportunities to break free from this cycle were elusive.

In the moments when the drug's influence was at its lowest, I clung to fragments of my former self, piecing together memories of who I was before this ordeal began. These memories, though fragmented, were a lifeline, a reminder that there was more to my existence than the savage battles I fought in the arena. They fueled a growing resolve to find a way out, to reclaim my freedom and humanity from the depths of this barbaric captivity.

Life in the Fighters' Cage

After proving myself in several brutal matches, I was moved to a larger cage, partitioned into smaller sections, offering something resembling privacy—a small luxury in the grim world of gladiatorial combat. The space wasn't much, but it allowed for a semblance of solitude. I shared this new living area with three other fighters, each marked by the horrors they had endured.

One of my new cellmates was severely battered, his body a map of scars, fresh cuts, and a missing eye—a testament to his recent battles. Another, a shorter man, had his head wrapped in a blood-soaked bandage. He didn't survive long; within hours of my arrival, he was dragged away. "Sold for meat," explained my third cellmate, indicating the grim fate of fighters who were no longer able to entertain the crowds.

This man, a hulking figure with a thick accent from north of the border, introduced himself as Vacarro. His tattoos revealed his past affiliation with one of the smaller cartels that had been absorbed by the dominant Azteco forces. Now, he too was caught in the brutal cycle of fight or be disposed of as mere meat.

"Only the strong matter here," Vacarro told me, his voice a mix of respect and resignation. He had noticed my ferocity in the arena. "You fight like a madman. That's why I speak to you. If you couldn't fight, I wouldn't care."

The conversation turned to the drugs—the white powder to prepare us for the red Fuego that fueled our rage in the arena. "Drugs still got you all messed up, huh?" Vacarro observed. I nodded, the effects of the substances lingering in my system, clouding my thoughts and perceptions.

"You get less of it now," he continued. "White stuff is to make you ready for the Fuego. Not everyone handles it well, but you, you turn into something else when you're on it."

His words made me reflect on the brutal reality of my existence here. Each fight was a desperate grasp at survival, a performance for the amusement of a crowd that thirsted for violence and spectacle. And as long as I continued to perform, I would live to see another day, trapped in this endless cycle of violence.

In the unforgiving world of the Azteco arenas, every fight was a desperate struggle for survival. Vaquero, a former cartel member turned gladiator, demonstrated his surprising agility and combat skills in a deadly match. Facing a massive opponent armed with a heavy chain, Vaquero's speed and strategic thinking came to the forefront. He deftly avoided a lethal swing aimed at decapitating him and closed the distance between himself and his adversary.

With a swift move, Vaquero grabbed the other fighter by his shirt and delivered a powerful headbutt, instantly breaking the man's nose. The impact dazed the opponent, causing him to drop his weapon—a heavy chain—which I quickly seized and used to entangle his legs. The chaos of the fight was palpable as both men grappled on the sandy floor of the arena, each blowing a potential death sentence.

The fight ended abruptly when the other gladiator, attempting to regain his footing, stumbled and fell backwards, his head striking a sharp rock concealed in the sand. The collision was fatal, and he lay motionless, blood pooling around his head. Vaquero stood over him, his expression one of confusion mixed with relief. He had survived another day in the brutal world of Azteco gladiators, but the victory was hollow. The realization that each fight could easily be his last was etched deeply into his features, a stark reminder of the harsh reality we both faced.

As we returned to our shared cage, the weight of our existence pressed heavily upon us. We were fighters in a world that valued our lives only as entertainment, our survival hanging by a thread. Each victory brought relief, but also a deeper understanding of the brutal cycle we were trapped in.

A Plan for Escape

Vaquero and I sat in our shared cell, surrounded by the modest luxuries granted to us as prized fighters. Despite the prime cuts of meat and fresh fruit piled before us, my mind was far from at ease. Vaquero, noticing my disinterest in the food, casually helped himself to my portions while we discussed our grim reality.

"You've been quiet, man. What's up?" Vaquero asked, his voice low, almost blending with the distant sounds of the arena's clamor.

I glanced at him, my thoughts still clouded by the lingering effects of the drugs, but sharpened by the memory of seeing Annie and Clay in the stands. "What are we going to do, Vaquero? Fight here until we die? I have people out there who need me," I confessed, the weight of my responsibilities pressing heavily on my chest.

Vaquero chuckled softly, peeling an orange with his large, calloused hands. "Okay, listen. I've been waiting for a partner like you. We can escape, but it's not a one-man job," he said, his voice serious.

"You mean you like me because I can fight?" I responded, half-joking to mask the desperation I felt.

"Yeah, sure, but no," Vaquero laughed, then leaned closer, lowering his voice. "I mean because you're smaller than me, you can fit."

"Fit where?" I asked, my curiosity piqued.

Vaquero's expression turned serious as he explained his plan. "There's a section of the arena, under the east stands. There's a drainage grate there. It's rusty and poorly guarded. I've noticed it because it's part of the route they take us through to the arena. I can't fit through it, but you... you might just make it."

The plan was risky, but it sparked a flicker of hope in my heart. Escape meant a chance to reunite with my people, to fight for a cause worth more than the entertainment of a bloodthirsty crowd. It was a slim chance, but it was the first real chance I'd had in what felt like forever.

As Vaquero and I plotted our escape, the reality of our situation set in. We were deep in enemy territory, surrounded by a society that thrived on violence and spectacle. But with each detail Vaquero outlined, my resolve hardened. We were not just gladiators; we were survivors, and we would do whatever it took to reclaim our freedom.

The drug known as Fuego coursed through me as I stepped into the arena, its fiery embrace as familiar as it was relentless. However, this time I had managed to hold my breath just enough to lessen its overwhelming grip. Clarity was crucial for what was to come.

Vaquero and I faced a pair of fighters as formidable as any we had encountered before. Their movements were swift and lethal, driven by the same drug-induced frenzy that fueled the arena's brutal spectacles. We fought back with everything we had, our every move, a dance between life and death.

The crowd roared with each clash of metal, their cheers fueled by the spectacle of violence unfolding before them. Yet, beneath the surface, a different kind of tension simmered between Vaquero and me. This fight wasn't just about survival; it was about securing our freedom.

As the fight drew to a bloody close, we emerged victorious, though not unscathed. My body ached from the exertion and the hits I'd taken, but the pain was overshadowed by the rush of relief at our win. We had earned another day of life, and more importantly, the opportunity to set our plan into motion.

Following the match, I approached the guard Vaquero had mentioned, my heart pounding with the weight of the moment. "I'd like to request a reward for tonight's victory," I said, my voice steady despite the adrenaline still coursing through me.

The guard eyed me suspiciously but nodded, aware that rewards were customary for those who entertained the masses so well. "What do you want?" he asked, his tone implying that nothing I requested should surprise him.

"A girl," I replied, the words tasting bitter in my mouth. It was part of the plan, a necessary evil to gain the guard's cooperation.

He smirked, a cruel twist to his lips, and motioned for me to follow. We walked to the holding cells where the slaves were kept, my stomach churning with each step. When he opened the door to the cells, I took a deep breath, preparing myself to face the horror inside and to pick someone who would play a pivotal role in our desperate bid for freedom.

The guard's back was to me as he unlocked one of the cells. That was when I gave the prearranged signal, a subtle nod that I hoped Annie, watching discreetly from the stands, would see. It was the signal that would bring my friends into play, the next crucial step in our harrowing escape plan.

An Unexpected Reunion

The arena's sun-bleached sands burned under my feet as the gates swung open, heralding another fight. Vaquero and I, now a seasoned team, were growing too familiar to the crowd. Their cheers, once exhilarating, now carried a note of bloodthirsty anticipation for our downfall.

As the opposing gate creaked open, four figures emerged, silhouetted against the harsh light. My heart pounded not just from the Fuego's fire in my veins but from a shock of recognition. Among them was Robert, my old mentor from the army days, looking haggard and wild, a makeshift spear clutched in his hand.

The crowd's roar drowned out any chance of communication. The Fuego coursing through us all ensured that any personal connections were temporarily severed, overridden by the primal urge to survive and conquer.

Vaquero and I positioned ourselves back to back, a tactic that had served us well in previous fights. But the odds were different this time. Four against two, and not just any two—my mentor was among them, driven by the same madness that fueled our survival in these brutal matches.

The initial clash was brutal. Spears and clubs swung through the air, aiming to maim or kill. Robert, under the influence of the Fuego, was a force of nature, his attacks relentless and driven by the same training that had once made him a protector.

As I dodged a lethal thrust from one of the other fighters, my mind raced. I needed to keep Robert alive, hoping that somehow, after the fight, I could reach out to him, remind him of who he was beyond the drug's influence.

Vaquero grappled with another fighter, using his massive strength to our advantage. I used the chaos to maneuver closer to Robert, trying to disarm rather than injure him. It was a dance of death, each move calculated with precision, yet hampered by the drug's haze clouding my judgment.

The crowd's excitement reached a fever pitch as the fight dragged on. Each move we made was met with roars of approval or boos of frustration, depending on whose blow landed or was deflected. In the frenzy, I managed to knock the spear from Robert's hands, sending it skittering across the sand.

For a brief moment, our eyes met. There was a flicker of recognition, or perhaps it was just my hope reflecting in his drug-dilated pupils. But the moment passed as quickly as it came, swallowed by the next wave of attacks.

Together, Vaquero and I managed to subdue the fighters without fatal blows—a difficult task, given the crowd's thirst for blood and the Fuego's push towards violence. When the guards finally declared the match over, the arena was filled with a mix of boos and cheers.

We were escorted back to our cage, bodies aching and hearts heavy. Robert was dragged in the opposite direction, his fate uncertain. As the gate of my cage clanged shut, I slumped against the cold metal, the Fuego's effects slowly ebbing away, leaving a deep, gnawing ache in its wake.

What had I become? What had we all become in this twisted new world where survival pitted friend against friend in a fight to the death? As I lay there, the weight of the day's events pressed down on me, a reminder of the brutal path that still lay ahead.

The Fuego's Grip

As Robert's second charge bore down on me, the Fuego's searing influence boiled my blood, sharpening every sense to a feral keenness. I could hear each ragged breath he took, see the sweat mingling with the paint on his face, and feel the heat radiating off his body as if the very air between us was aflame.

Dodging another of his frenzied swings, I managed to maneuver behind him, reaching out to grab his shoulders in a desperate attempt to pin him. But he was too fueled by the Fuego; his body twisted with a violent jerk, throwing me off balance. As I stumbled, he spun around, his fists ready to continue the assault.

The crowd was a roaring entity of its own, their cries and cheers feeding the madness of the combat. Each shout seemed to drive Robert further into his frenzy, their energy fueling his relentless attacks.

Vaquero, seeing my struggle, tried to intervene, swinging his sledgehammer in a wide arc to keep the other fighters at bay while I dealt with Robert. His weapon was a blur of motion, creating a deadly perimeter around us.

I ducked under another wild punch from Robert, feeling the air shift above my head. The reality of fighting him—the man who had once been a mentor and friend—was heart-wrenching. With each evasion, I called out to him, each plea drowned out by the cacophony of the crowd and the blood rushing in my ears.

"Robert, it's me! Remember who you are!" My voice cracked under the strain, the Fuego gnawing at my resolve, urging me to fight back with lethal intent.

But then, in a moment of unexpected clarity amidst the chaos, our eyes met. Something flickered in his gaze—a distant recognition, a confusion that battled the drug's hold. It was a fleeting connection, soon lost as another gladiator's interference pulled my attention away.

I was forced to engage the new threat, a burly man wielding a spiked club. As I parried and struck, the fight with Robert had shifted. He seemed momentarily stalled, his actions hesitant as if fighting against Fuego's influence.

Taking advantage of the moment, I pushed the attacking gladiator back with a series of rapid movements, my training overcoming the drug's disorienting effects. My mind raced, trying to formulate a plan that could save both Robert and myself from this barbaric end.

The fight wore on, each second stretching into eternity as sand and sweat mingled on my skin. Vaquero's hammer found its mark again, and another opponent crumpled to the ground, leaving us facing the remaining fighters who hesitated, seeing their numbers dwindling.

As the dust settled, and the crowd's roar dimmed slightly, I turned back to Robert, who was watching me with a mix of confusion and dawning awareness. The battle wasn't just in the arena; it was in his mind, fighting against Fuego's corrosive touch.

"Robert," I said softly, stepping closer, my hands raised in a gesture of peace. "We don't have to do this. Remember who you are, who I am. We're not enemies."

His breathing was heavy, his fists still clenched, but his stance was less aggressive, more uncertain. It was a small victory, perhaps the first step in breaking Fuego's hold, but around us, the arena demanded more blood, and the fight was far from over.

A Clash of Titans and Torn Loyalties

Robert sprang to his feet and quickly retrieved one of the discarded cestus gloves from the ground. His movements were agile, betraying his combat experience, despite the influence of the Fuego. I watched him cautiously, recognizing the signs of his fading rage. It was a brief window, a moment where the drug's grip loosened just enough to allow the real Robert—a soldier, a mentor, a friend—to peer through the haze of battle frenzy.

My own body ached from the fight, the Fuego's effects ebbing slowly, leaving behind a raw clarity. I was panting, feeling the cuts and bruises that painted my body with throbbing pain. As we circled each other, the crowd's roar seemed to diminish into a distant echo, the world narrowing down to the space between Robert and me.

"Robert, listen to me," I tried again, my voice hoarse but firm. "You know me. I'm not your enemy. We don't have to do this."

He hesitated, his grip on the cestus tightening, then loosening slightly. The confusion was evident in his eyes, warring with the lingering effects of the drug. "I... I don't want to fight you," he muttered, almost to himself, his voice barely audible over the crowd.

"You don't have to," I said, taking a cautious step towards him. "We can find another way. Think about your family, think about what you're fighting for."

Robert's eyes flickered with recognition, then doubt. The internal struggle was visible, a man fighting against his own drug-induced nature. "My family..." he whispered, his stance relaxing slightly.

Seizing the moment, I closed the distance between us, lowering my voice so only he could hear. "Yes, your family. Remember who you are, Robert. You're not a killer. You're a protector. Let's end this madness."

For a moment, it seemed like he would give in, his eyes clearing as he met my gaze. Then, a shadow passed over his features, a reminder of the drug's persistent call. With a grunt of frustration, he swung the cestus, an instinctive response to the relentless pull of the Fuego. I dodged, feeling the air shift beside my head, the miss as close as it could get without drawing blood.

"We don't have to be enemies," I pressed, dodging another swing. "Think of your family, think of mine. We're not just fighters in an arena. We're more than this."

Robert paused, his breathing heavy, his gaze locked on mine. The battle raged around us, other fighters clashing in the sandy pit, but in our little circle, a different kind of fight was taking place— a battle for a man's soul against the darkness of the Fuego.

As the crowd screamed for blood and violence, for a moment, just a fleeting moment, I saw the man Robert once was. The mentor, the soldier, the protector. And in that moment, I knew there was still hope for him, for us, despite the odds stacked against us in this brutal, forgotten corner of the world.

A Plot for Freedom

I explained our plan in a quiet, urgent whisper, telling Annie and Clay about the loose bars Vaquero had managed to work on. The look in Annie's eyes was hard to read, but I saw determination there, and maybe a hint of fear. "We only have a small window during the next fight to make this work," I said. "When they take me to the arena, you and Clay need to be ready."

Clay, who had been mostly silent up until now, nodded. "We'll be there. I've seen enough to know I don't want any part of this place longer than I have to be."

Annie squeezed my hand through the bars, her grip strong despite the coolness of her skin. "We'll make sure everything's ready on our end. Just... just make sure you come back to us. Don't get caught up in the frenzy."

I nodded, understanding her unspoken words. The Fuego made it hard to control myself, but I knew what was at stake. "I'll be careful," I promised, though I knew it was a promise that would be hard to keep.

The next day, as the sun began to set, the familiar adrenaline started to build up in me, but it was different this time. It wasn't just the pre-fight nerves or the drug; it was the hope of escape, the possibility of seeing the outside world again, of breathing air not filled with the scent of blood and fear.

Vaquero clapped me on the back as we were led to the arena. "Today's the day, hermano," he said, his voice a low rumble. "Make it count."

The arena was packed as usual, the crowd buzzing with anticipation. I could feel their eyes on me, the weight of their expectations pressing down. But today, I wasn't just fighting for their entertainment. I was fighting for my freedom.

As the gate lifted, I stepped into the arena, my eyes scanning for Annie and Clay in the stands. They were there, just as we had planned, looking tense and ready. Across the sand, my opponents waited, looking just as determined and deadly as ever.

But this fight was different. Every move I made was calculated, every step taken with the escape plan in mind. When the moment came, as Vaquero engaged the last of our opponents in a feint to draw attention, I made a break for the edge of the arena, towards a section we knew was poorly monitored.

Heart pounding, I reached the wall and began to climb, the rough stones scraping my palms. Below me, the crowd erupted into chaos as they realized what was happening. Shouts filled the air, a mixture of cheers and boos, but I didn't look back. I couldn't.

Reaching the top of the wall, I threw myself over, rolling to absorb the impact on the other side. I was out, but I wasn't safe yet. I sprinted towards the meeting point, my lungs burning with each breath.

Behind me, the arena was a storm of noise and movement, but ahead was the promise of freedom. And there, just as we had planned, were Annie and Clay, their faces a sight for sore eyes.

"We did it," I gasped, nearly collapsing into their arms. "We actually did it."

Annie hugged me tightly, relief and joy mingling on her face. "Let's get out of here," she said, pulling me along. "Before they realize you're gone."

Together, we ran, leaving the shouts and the chaos of the arena behind us, racing towards a future that was suddenly full of possibilities.

The Final Countdown

The fights were temporarily paused due to a major festival the Aztecos were preparing. This unusual break provided us a critical chance to rest and finalize our escape plans. During this time, Vaquero and I stayed mostly in our cage, conserving energy and avoiding unnecessary attention. We spoke in hushed tones about what was to come, rehearsing every step of our planned escape.

The night before our planned escape, Vaquero seemed more serious than usual. "Listen," he said quietly, "if anything goes wrong, you keep going. Don't stop for anything."

I nodded, understanding the gravity of his words. "And you?"

"I'll cover you as long as I can," he replied, clapping a heavy hand on my shoulder. "We've got one shot at this, don't waste it."

That night, I hardly slept. The weight of what was to come pressed heavily on me. I thought about Annie, Clay, and the life I was fighting to return to. The stakes were high, not just for me, but for everyone involved.

Day 759 arrived, the darkest night of the month. As we prepared, I felt the familiar fear creeping up, mixed with an adrenaline-fueled readiness. We were given our usual dose of Fuego, but I managed to spit most of it out when the guards weren't looking. I needed clarity for what was about to happen.

The guards led us to the arena for what was supposed to be a standard fight, but we knew it was anything but. The crowd was thinner, the night darker, and the air filled with an electric tension. As we entered the arena, Vaquero gave me a nod, the signal that it was time.

Midway through the fight, when we had maneuvered ourselves close to the lesser-guarded eastern wall of the arena, Vaquero shouted a distraction and threw a heavy punch at the wall. The impact was louder than expected, drawing the attention of the guards. In that moment, I ran towards the loose bars we'd prepared earlier.

Pulling with all the strength I could muster, I managed to widen the gap just enough to squeeze through. Heart pounding, I slipped through the bars and landed on the other side. I didn't look back; I couldn't. Vaquero's shouts echoed behind me, a chaotic blend of pain and defiance.

Running as fast as my legs would carry me, I headed for the pre-arranged meeting point. The darkness was a blessing, shrouding my escape as I dodged between shadows and buildings. Behind me, the sounds of the arena grew fainter, replaced by the pounding of my own heart in my ears.

After what felt like an eternity, I spotted the faint outline of Annie and Clay waiting by the old truck we had stashed days earlier. Relief washed over me as I approached, but it was quickly replaced by a surge of urgency.

"We have to go, now!" I gasped, my breath ragged.

Annie wasted no time, pulling me into the truck while Clay jumped into the driver's seat. The engine roared to life, and we sped away into the night, the lights of the Azteco settlement fading behind us.

As we put distance between ourselves and the arena, the reality of our escape began to sink in. We were free, at least for now. But our thoughts were with Vaquero, left behind to face whatever consequences would come from our escape.

"We'll find a way to help him," Annie said firmly, her voice cutting through the darkness. "We're not done yet."

I nodded, the weight of her words settling heavy on my shoulders. We had escaped, but our fight was far from over.

During the nights leading up to the new moon, the Aztecos were noticeably apprehensive, adhering to their superstitions by staying indoors and avoiding unnecessary ventures into the darkness. This presented an optimal opportunity for our escape. Vaquero and I knew our time as champions in the arena was running out. The crowd's interest was waning, and the organizers would soon arrange for us to face insurmountable odds. We needed to act while we still had strength left to fight.

On the night of the new moon, the arena compound was quieter than usual, with only the minimal number of guards on duty, reflecting the general unease that accompanied this phase of the moon. After the guards completed their final rounds checking the cells, they settled into their usual routine in the small guard hut, either dozing off or distracted by a game of cards.

Taking advantage of the quiet, I squeezed through the bars that Vaquero had managed to loosen over the past weeks. Stealthily, I approached the hut where the guards kept the keys to the cells. The window, poorly secured, provided just enough space for me to reach in and grab the keys without alerting the guards inside.

With the keys in hand, I hurried back to our cage to release Vaquero. Our next steps had to be swift and silent—we couldn't afford any delays. Once Vaquero was free, we quickly moved to the adjacent cages to release the other fighters. Many were too weak or scared to fight, but a few were like us, waiting for a chance to strike back or escape.

As Vaquero and I freed the other capable fighters, we whispered a simple plan: cause as much chaos as possible to cover our escape. We armed ourselves with whatever makeshift weapons we could find—pieces of metal, broken chains, and even stones.

With a group of about a dozen fighters, we surged towards the main gate of the compound. The guards, surprised by our sudden rebellion and numbed by the superstitions of the new moon, were slow to respond. We overwhelmed them quickly, using our sheer numbers and the element of surprise to our advantage.

The night air was cool and filled with the smell of rain—a stark contrast to the hot, dusty arena we had just fled. As we ran into the darkness, the sound of alarms began to fill the air behind us. Searchlights swept the grounds, and shouts echoed as the compound stirred to life, awakened from its new moon slumber.

We didn't stop running until we were well beyond the reach of the searchlights, deep into the woods surrounding the compound. The darkness of the new moon provided the perfect cover, and the rain helped mask our tracks. We knew the Aztecos would pursue us, but we also knew the terrain better than they did, and we had the cover of darkness on our side.

Exhausted but free, we huddled together in the woods, catching our breath and planning our next move. We were out of the arena but not out of danger. We needed to find a way to get back to Farmbridge, to warn them of the Aztecos' strength and ruthlessness, and to bring help for those we had left behind.

As the first light of dawn began to break, we set off again, determined to put as much distance as possible between us and the Azteco compound. Our journey back to safety was just beginning, but for the first time in a long while, there was a spark of hope. We were no longer just survivors of the arena; we were fighters, and we were free.

After setting the fire, I felt a surge of adrenaline mixed with a profound sense of finality. Vaquero gripped my arm tightly, pulling me away from the growing inferno. "We need to move now!" he urged, his voice a mix of fear and determination. The town was erupting into chaos, with the freed gladiators causing havoc and the fire spreading quickly through the closely packed houses.

We darted through the narrow alleyways, dodging both the frantic townspeople and the increasingly aggressive Azteco guards who were struggling to maintain order. The smoke from the fire filled the air, stinging our eyes and throats, but also providing cover as we made our way to the outskirts of town.

Annie and Clay were waiting for us at a pre-arranged meeting spot, hidden in the dense brush near the town's edge. They had managed to secure a small, battered vehicle—barely more than a rusty shell on wheels, but it was our ticket out of there. Annie looked relieved but shocked as we approached. "You started that fire?" she asked, her voice tinged with disbelief and worry.

I nodded, unable to muster a verbal response, the gravity of what I had done settling in. Clay worked quickly to remove our collars with the pliers he'd brought, tossing them aside with a clatter.

"We don't have much time," he said. "They'll organize and come after us once they realize what's happened."

With the collars removed, we piled into the vehicle. Vaquero took the driver's seat, his large frame barely fitting behind the steering wheel. As we bounced along the uneven road leading away from the town, I looked back at the rising plumes of smoke. The town, a stronghold of horror and oppression, was now engulfed in flames—a stark symbol of the anarchy the Aztecos had brought upon themselves.

The drive was tense, with every bump and noise causing us to flinch, expecting pursuit. But as the miles stretched on and the smoke faded into the distance, the immediate fear of being chased waned. Instead, a deep fatigue set in. We had escaped, but at what cost? The town was likely in ruins, many would die—innocent or not. The complexity of our actions weighed heavily on me.

Annie broke the silence as we neared the border. "What now?" she asked, her eyes searching mine for a plan. I met her gaze, feeling the responsibility of our next steps. "We head back to Farmbridge," I said. "We warn them, we prepare. The Aztecos won't stop with that town, and neither can we."

Days 769-773 were spent making our way back to Farmbridge. Despite our escape, the journey was fraught with hazards. The fallout of our actions at the town had sent ripples through the region, and we encountered several patrols. However, our disguises and the general confusion helped us avoid detection.

When we finally saw the familiar outlines of Farmbridge, a wave of relief washed over me. We had made it back. But as we approached the gates, the real work lay ahead. We had to convince everyone of the looming threat, unify the settlements, and prepare for what was coming. The road ahead was uncertain, but one thing was clear: together, we had a fighting chance.

The village was quiet as we approached it, eerily so. The kind faces that had welcomed us months ago were absent, replaced by a tense air of suspicion and fear. As we drew closer, an old woman recognized us, her expression turning from surprise to distress. She hurriedly gestured for us to follow her to a secluded spot by the water's edge.

"Things have changed," she whispered hurriedly once we were out of earshot of the rest. "After you left, the Aztecos came. They took many as slaves, and those who resisted..." Her voice trailed off, and she didn't need to finish her sentence; the haunted look in her eyes said it all.

"We're so sorry," Annie replied, her voice thick with guilt. "Our actions put you all in danger."

The woman shook her head slowly. "No, child. It was our choice to help you. But now, you must be careful. They have been patrolling the waters. If they find you here, they will not hesitate."

We exchanged looks, the weight of her words settling heavily upon us. We couldn't stay long. "We need supplies," Clay said quietly, "just enough to get us moving again."

The old woman nodded and quickly organized a few villagers to gather what little they could spare—some food, water, and a few medical supplies. As we prepared to leave, she gripped my arm. "Go, and do not return here. It is too dangerous now. May the spirits protect you."

Days 780-784 were spent making our way north, sticking to the coastline to avoid the main roads where Azteco patrols were most frequent. Our progress was slow; the need for caution limited our travel to the night hours. We encountered a few deserted villages along the way, the remnants of Azteco raids visible in the charred structures and abandoned homes. It was a grim reminder of the devastation these raiders could unleash.

As we neared the outskirts of Farmbridge, the reality of what we'd have to explain and the alliances we'd need to forge weighed heavily on us. The first glimpses of familiar territory brought both relief and a renewed sense of urgency.

"We need a plan," I said as we huddled together one evening, the lights of Farmbridge visible in the distance. "We can't just walk in there without proof or a solid strategy. They need to be prepared for what's coming."

Annie nodded in agreement. "I'll go ahead first," she offered. "Gauge the situation, see how they've been holding up, and set up a meeting with Ruslana and the others."

Vaquero clapped a heavy hand on my shoulder, his voice low and serious. "We did good today, amigo. We survived. Now, we make sure everyone else does too."

With a plan in place and our resolve strengthened, we approached Farmbridge, ready to face whatever came next, prepared to fight not just for our survival, but for the future of all those threatened by the Azteco menace.

The Return Journey and Reflections

Days 780 to 785 found us trekking through the desolate expanses of the Northwestern Mexican wastes, a place seemingly forsaken by both man and nature. With the Azteco territory behind us, our immediate fears of encountering their brutal patrols diminished, but the landscape itself posed its own threats. The harsh terrain, dotted with the remnants of once-thriving communities, served as a stark reminder of the widespread devastation.

During these days, our group was enveloped in a silence born from exhaustion and reflection. Each of us was lost in our own thoughts, processing the horrors we had witnessed and the roles we had played. The weight of our actions, particularly my own in sparking the tragic events at the village, lay heavily upon me.

One evening, as we made camp in the shelter of a crumbling adobe wall, Annie broke the silence. "We need to make plans for when we get back," she said, her voice cutting through the stillness. "It's not just about surviving anymore. It's about what comes next, how we help those who are left."

I nodded, feeling the truth of her words. "We have a lot to do. Informing Farmbridge about the Aztecos, securing more allies, maybe even warning The Iron Lady's territory about what's coming. They might be our enemies, but they're also in danger."

Vaquero chimed in, his tone somber yet determined. "We can't let what happened to those villagers happen to others. We might not like The Iron Lady, but if her forces are decimated by the Aztecos, that's just opening the door for them to push further north."

Clay, who had been quietly tuning an old radio, looked up. "There's also the matter of the veterans at the armory. They have the resources we desperately need. We have to convince them to join us, not just for our sake but for everyone's."

The conversation continued into the night, each of us contributing ideas and potential strategies. Despite the grim circumstances, there was a sense of purpose that hadn't been there before. We were no longer just survivors, but defenders. As we laid out our plans under the vast, starlit sky, a renewed sense of hope began to take root. Maybe, just maybe, we could make a difference.

The Long Road Home

Days 786-790 brought us to the old U.S.-Mexico border. The atmosphere among our group was a mix of relief and trepidation as we prepared to cross into what was once familiar territory, now marked by the scars of past conflicts. The evening before we crossed, Vaquero and I stood watch together, the quiet of the desert around us lending itself to reflection and candid conversations.

"Vaquero, what are your plans when we get back north?" I asked, breaking the silence.

Vaquero looked out into the dark expanse, the stars faintly illuminating his thoughtful expression. "Survive, I guess," he began slowly. "Do what I always do—rob, raid, steal. Whatever it takes to keep going until I can't anymore."

His response was a stark reminder of the different paths we had before us. "You know, Farmbridge and the other communities —they're different. They have order, rules... a system. There's a place for someone like you there," I suggested, hoping to steer him towards a less solitary and destructive path.

Vaquero scoffed lightly, shaking his head. "Nah, vato. That old world stuff—laws, order—it ain't for me. I'll find my own way, far from all that."

I respected his choice, though it pained me to think of him continuing a life of solitude and conflict. "And you? What will you do with your time?" he asked, turning the question back on me.

His question caught me off guard. I had been so focused on surviving and escaping that I hadn't allowed myself to think about what came next. Before I could answer, Vaquero continued, "You know about the Fuego, right? Use it enough, and it messes you up. Turns your brain to mush. Makes you into a monster, all the time, not just when you're high."

I nodded silently, the weight of his words sinking in. The Fuego had been a tool for survival in the arenas, but the long-term effects were devastating.

"We call them zombies," Vaquero added, a hint of dark humor in his tone.

The conversation lingered in my mind as we resumed our journey the following morning. The crossing was uneventful, but the real challenges awaited us as we approached familiar lands, carrying not just the scars of our physical battles but the deeper, unseen marks left by our experiences. The road home was long, and it promised to be just as arduous as any fight we had faced in the arenas of the Azteco territory.

Days 786-792 were marked by our cautious approach to Farm Bridge. The fertile fields that surrounded the community had expanded, a sign of growth and prosperity. Our presence was quickly noticed by a patrol in a desert-painted Humvee, an upgrade from the last time I'd seen the community's defenses. They recognized us immediately and escorted us to the community center.

As we approached, the familiar sights of Farm Bridge were both comforting and surreal. The community had not only survived but thrived, adapting to the new world with resilience and ingenuity. I was overwhelmed with emotion, a mixture of relief to be back and anxiety about the future.

We were quickly ushered into a meeting with the community leaders, where I shared the harrowing details of our experiences in Azteco territory. The room was silent as I spoke of the Fuego's lasting effects and my fears for those who had been exposed. The leaders listened intently, their faces etched with concern.

After the meeting, I found myself alone for a moment, staring out at the expanded fields, reflecting on everything that had happened. It was here that Annie found me, her presence a silent support. We didn't speak much; instead, we shared a moment of quiet understanding. The battles we had fought were behind us, but the war for our souls and the future of this new world was just beginning.

That night, as I lay in a familiar bed in Farm Bridge, the faces of those I had lost and those I had saved haunted my dreams. The weight of the past and the uncertainty of the future mingled in my restless thoughts. I knew that the road ahead would be fraught with challenges, but for the first time in a long time, I felt like I was where I needed to be.

Days 793 to 795 unfolded under the comforting familiarity of Farm Bridge. Lucky, ever loyal, had become my constant shadow, his presence a comforting reassurance as I navigated my return to a semblance of normalcy. Each day, I took long walks around the community, Lucky trotting beside me, and I was struck by the transformations that had occurred in my absence.

The fields were greener, larger, and the sounds of children playing were frequent—a stark contrast to the silence of the barren landscapes I had left behind. The community had expanded, new faces mingling with the old, and the sense of purpose that drove everyone was palpable. They were not just surviving; they were thriving, building something lasting.

My evenings were spent around the campfire with old friends and new acquaintances. Stories were exchanged—tales of bravery, loss, and resilience. I shared my own stories, too, though I carefully curated the horrors I had witnessed, not wanting to bring the shadows of my recent past into the light of our present gatherings.

Christina and I found time to talk, away from the others. Our conversation was a tentative dance around the scars we both carried—hers visible in her wary eyes, mine hidden deep within. We spoke of forgiveness and futures, though neither of us was sure what either would look like.

As for Alexis, our reconnection was a slow rebuilding of trust. The joy of our reunion was tempered by the unspoken fears and uncertainties that lay between us. We took each day as it came, learning to navigate our new realities together.

The days at Farm Bridge passed with a gentle rhythm, a stark contrast to the chaos of my previous life. Yet, even in this peace, I couldn't shake the feeling of being a storm-chaser at heart— always aware that calm surfaces often belie the deepest currents.

Days of Preparation and Political Unrest at Farm Bridge

Days 796 to 799 at Farm Bridge marked a significant turn in the community's history as it, along with its allied settlements, began shaping a formal coalition known as the California Republic. This newfound union, born from the ashes of nuclear devastation and the constant threats from external forces like the Aztecos and the Army of the Dawn, was a testament to the resilience and determination of these communities.

Annie's successful communication had played a crucial role. Her messenger had not only brought back crucial intelligence but had also stirred a sense of urgency within the coalition. Now, with Clay's group back and integrating their firsthand experiences with the Aztecos into the community's defense plans, there was a real sense of momentum.

As representatives from other Californian settlements made their way to Farm Bridge, the atmosphere was charged with a mix of hope and determination. Meetings were held daily, with discussions focusing on defense strategies, resource sharing, and potential diplomatic approaches to handle the threats.

Meanwhile, the scars of my recent past remained both visible on my skin and hidden within the depths of my psyche. The nights were particularly tough, as the remnants of Fuego haunted my dreams, leaving me restless. Alexis and Lucky provided comfort, their presence a constant reassurance of the life I fought to return to. However, the quiet moments of reflection reminded me of the internal battles that awaited me, the psychological remnants of my ordeal as vivid as the physical scars that marked my body.

These days at Farm Bridge were not just a respite but a preparation for the inevitable conflicts that lay ahead. As the community braced itself for potential confrontations, my own fight for personal peace and reconciliation with my past actions continued unabated, shadowing the communal efforts to forge a safer future.

Day 800 at Farm Bridge unfolded with a mixture of anticipation and apprehension as a motorcade approached, signaling significant arrivals. The convoy, a long procession that stirred dust and curiosity, included vehicles recognizable as part of Clay's group. A sense of cautious optimism pervaded the air as this signaled not just the reunion of community members but also the return of resources and perhaps additional support.

However, the atmosphere quickly shifted as a U.S. Army Striker rolled into view, adorned with the emblem of the Army of Dawn. The sight was jarring—the fresh paint on the emblem a stark reminder of the looming presence and influence of the Iron Lady. As the convoy halted within the gates of Farm Bridge, the community's focus turned to this unexpected guest.

The Iron Lady emerged from the Striker with a calculated calm that contrasted sharply with the undercurrents of tension her presence generated. Her gaze swept over Farm Bridge, taking in the thriving community, the new structures, and the gathering crowd, before locking eyes with me. In that moment, time seemed to stand still, as her arrival brought with it the complexities of past alliances, conflicts, and the overarching struggle between the emerging California Republic's ideals and her own authoritarian rule.

This pivotal moment was not just a simple arrival; it was a convergence of past conflicts and current uncertainties, raising questions about motives, alliances, and the potential shifts in power dynamics within the newly forming political landscape of the California Republic.

CHAPTER 6: TENSE NEGOTIATIONS AT THE CALIFORNIA REPUBLIC CONGRESS

Day 900 marked a critical juncture for the nascent California Republic, with Farm Bridge hosting an essential congress of settlement leaders. The Iron Lady's presence was both a stark reminder of external threats and a testament to the complex dynamics at play. The meeting hall, repurposed from Farm Bridge's largest communal building, was tense, filled with the leaders of various settlements who had united under the banner of the California Republic to resist both the Aztecos' chaos and the Iron Lady's authoritarian rule.

As Ruslana opened the session, her leadership was evident, though she remained just one voice among many in a government that prized collective decision-making. She had adapted from her days as a military strategist to a peacemaker and leader in a post-apocalyptic society, emphasizing democracy and cooperation over hierarchy and dominance.

The Iron Lady, meanwhile, assessed the room with a calculated gaze. Despite her reduced security detail, her demeanor was composed, exuding a quiet confidence that belied her current vulnerable position. Her presence at this congress was strategic, necessitated by the greater threats that even she could not ignore and the potential benefits of forming alliances rather than waging costly wars.

The discussions that unfolded were cautious, with each representative weighing their words, aware that they were not just addressing their peers but also negotiating with a formidable adversary in their midst. Topics ranged from resource allocation and mutual defense to the potential integration of the Iron Lady's forces into the Republic's military framework under strict terms that would ensure the Republic's values remained intact.

The stakes were incredibly high. As proposals were debated, it was clear that every decision could tip the fragile balance between peace and conflict. The Republic's leaders were not just planning for immediate threats but also laying the groundwork for a future governance structure that could withstand the challenges of a post-nuclear world.

This congress was not merely a meeting; it was a pivotal moment in the California Republic's history, determining whether it could truly forge a new path forward or if the old world's shadows would dictate its future.

As The Iron Lady stood firmly before the congress, her tone was direct and devoid of any diplomacy, reflecting the urgency of her message. She addressed the assembled leaders, cutting through the rising noise of dissent. "Yes, they'll wipe us out, break themselves like you said, but they'll be weakened. They'll need time to recover, and in that time, what will stop them from turning west? You? With what army? We're the buffer right now, and without us, you're next."

Her words, stern and unyielding, hung heavily in the air. A nervous silence followed, punctuated only by the soft rustling of people shifting uncomfortably in their seats. The Iron Lady's gaze swept across the room, her eyes piercing each leader, daring them to challenge her logic.

Ruslana took this moment to rise, her presence commanding attention. "While I don't share The Iron Lady's methods or her past leadership style, I must concede her point on this matter. We cannot afford to let them consume her forces and then turn their sights on us. We're not ready to face such a horde alone."

The room buzzed with whispered conversations as leaders considered the gravity of the situation. The debate that ensued was heated, with voices raised not just in fear but also in strategic calculation. Some argued for bolstering defenses, others suggested sending aid to The Iron Lady's forces to ensure they could continue to act as a shield.

Finally, a consensus began to emerge. It was agreed that a contingent of volunteers would be sent to aid The Iron Lady, not as a sign of submission but as a tactical move to buy time for the California Republic to strengthen its own defenses. Additionally, plans were made to send scouts east to gather intelligence and assess the true strength of the enemy.

As the congress adjourned, there was a palpable sense of uneasy alliance in the air. It was a decision made not out of trust, but out of necessity, a strategic gambit in a world where the balance of power was constantly shifting and survival was never guaranteed.

Strategic Discussions and Plans Against the Aztecos

As the California Republic's congress continued to deliberate, the urgency to address the threat posed by the Aztecos grew. I attended numerous meetings, presenting the grim details of the enemy's capabilities and the atrocities I had witnessed. My testimony, corroborated by Clay and Annie, gradually shifted the tide of opinion among the representatives.

The debates were long and fraught with concerns about sovereignty and the fear of submitting to The Iron Lady's command. However, the consensus was clear: the existential threat of the Aztecos required a unified response. "We need to act now," I urged in one session, "not just with soldiers and weapons, but with a strategy that ensures we're not just surviving today but securing tomorrow."

A plan began to take shape, focusing on several key actions:

1. **Intelligence Gathering:** Enhanced reconnaissance missions would be conducted to monitor Azteco movements and gather detailed intelligence on their numbers, weaponry, and tactics.

2. **Fortification of Borders:** Resources would be allocated to strengthen defenses along the most vulnerable parts of the republic's territory, particularly areas closest to the Azteco-controlled regions.

3. **Training and Equipping Militias:** Local militias would receive training and supplies from the central armory, ensuring that even the smallest settlements could defend themselves.

4. **Diplomatic Efforts:** Attempts would be made to reach out to other survivor groups and former enemies to bolster the numbers of the allied forces.

Each point was debated intensely. Leaders worried about the strain on their resources and the political implications of aligning too closely with The Iron Lady. However, the stark reality of the threat pressed them to agree on a course of action.

"We're not just fighting for today," I concluded in one of the final meetings. "We're fighting for the chance to rebuild a world where our children can live without fear of being dragged into the darkness of a warlord's ambitions."

With a plan in place, the focus shifted to implementation. Logistics teams worked on supply routes, engineers drafted blueprints for new fortifications, and trainers scheduled sessions for the militias. The atmosphere was charged with a sense of purpose, a collective effort to forge a future from the chaos of the post-apocalyptic world.

Uniting Against the Azteco Threat

During a pivotal session with Ruslana and the leaders of the most influential settlements within the California Republic, the conversation focused intensely on the collective defense strategy against the Aztecos. I was asked to share my firsthand experiences and assessments regarding the viability of standing alone against such a formidable enemy.

"Alone, each of our settlements is vulnerable," I stated firmly to the assembly. "The Aztecos do not just outnumber us; they bring a brutality and fanaticism that none of us can withstand in isolation."

The room was thick with tension as leaders weighed the reality of our situation against their desire for autonomy. The decision to unify forces under a central command was fraught with political implications, but the existential threat looming just beyond our borders pushed the assembly towards consensus.

"The Iron Lady has the military experience and the resources,"

I continued, "but she needs our numbers, our local knowledge, and our will to fight."

After hours of discussions, a vote was taken. The result was overwhelmingly in favor of a united front, not just in military terms but also in pooling resources for intelligence and logistics, fortifying mutual defenses, and establishing a framework for sharing technological and medical advancements.

The agreement was dubbed the **SoCal Defense Pact**, and detailed plans were drawn up for rapid implementation. Training schedules were set, supply lines established, and defensive perimeters strengthened. Each settlement contributed what they could, from manpower to munitions, to ensure that when the Aztecos came, they would meet a well-prepared and united force.

As the meeting adjourned, there was a palpable sense of both relief and foreboding. We had taken a significant step toward survival, but the road ahead was fraught with danger. The real test of our newly formed alliance would come when the Aztecos advanced, and how well we could hold together under the pressures of war. Meanwhile, I couldn't help but wonder about the personal toll the impending conflict would take, not just on me but on all those I had come to care about in this harsh new world.

As the California Republic faced the daunting task of gearing up for war, Ruslana's strategic decision to delay the deployment of our forces for intensive training was met with mixed reactions. While The Iron Lady expressed frustration over the delay, emphasizing the urgency of support, Ruslana stood firm on her stance, prioritizing the readiness and survival of her troops over hasty actions.

During a critical meeting aimed at addressing the dire ammunition shortage, all participants recognized the severity of the situation. The discussion turned tense as Johnson, a seasoned special forces veteran now leading one of the major militias within the Republic, outlined the stark realities of our logistical capabilities.

"We've scoured every depot within reach," Johnson explained, his voice grim. "What little we found has been allocated to immediate defense needs. There's simply not enough to sustain prolonged combat, especially if we face an enemy equipped with similar heavy weaponry."

The room fell silent, the gravity of his words weighing heavily on every leader present. Without sufficient ammunition, even the best-trained forces would be at a severe disadvantage, potentially altering the outcome of the conflict.

Ruslana, ever the strategist, then proposed a bold move. "We need to initiate a salvage operation. There are rumored caches left by the U.S. military in several remote locations. It's a long shot, but we might find the supplies we need."

The plan was risky, involving reconnaissance teams venturing into uncharted territories that were potentially hazardous or enemy-controlled. However, the alternative—facing the Aztecos under-equipped—was unthinkable.

Clay, representing the technical and logistical teams, added, "We'll need to outfit squads with the best available gear and ensure they have enough support to make it back. It's not just about finding the ammo; it's about bringing it home."

The decision was made. Teams were quickly assembled, each

tasked with investigating different locations where the caches were believed to be hidden. The operations were set to commence immediately, with the understanding that every hour counted.

As the meeting adjourned, the leaders dispersed, each aware that the coming days would likely determine the fate of their newly formed Republic. The tension of impending conflict mingled with a flicker of hope—hope that these efforts would fortify their defenses enough to withstand whatever lay ahead.

As the critical strategy meeting unfolded, Ruslana intervened between two seasoned veterans, Johnson and The Iron Lady, both of whom were steeped in a military background possibly touching on black ops. The tension was palpable as they discussed the dire ammunition shortage that threatened their preparedness against the encroaching Azteco threat.

Ruslana proposed a bold yet controversial plan to approach a heavily armed settlement in Indian Springs, known for its hostility towards outsiders. "Traders have reported that the Army and Air Force left behind significant stockpiles when they abandoned the area," Ruslana explained, suggesting a diplomatic approach despite the settlement's aggressive reputation.

The Iron Lady, always strategic and calculating, suggested an alternative if diplomacy failed. "If they are as isolated and hostile as you say, then perhaps a show of strength is necessary. A joint operation could serve as a pivotal moment to solidify our alliance and demonstrate our collective strength," she proposed, her voice carrying both command and a hint of inevitability.

Alexis stood up, visibly shaken by the suggestion of using force. "Absolutely not! That's not who we are," she exclaimed, her voice trembling with emotion. Her reaction highlighted the moral dilemmas faced by the leaders of the California Republic, caught between survival and their values.

Ruslana paused, considering the gravity of the decision. Her eyes shifted across the room, measuring the reaction of each representative. The room was a mix of resolute and uneasy faces, each leader wrestling with the prospect of initiating conflict as a preemptive measure.

The debate continued, with various leaders voicing their concerns and strategic insights. The discussion was not just about logistics and military tactics, but also about the principles upon which the new republic would stand. Would they become the very threat they aimed to oppose, or find a path that aligned with their ideals of democracy and cooperation?

As the meeting adjourned, the weight of their decisions loomed large. Whatever course they chose, it was clear that the path forward would be fraught with challenges both from within and without. The Republic stood at a crossroads, and the next steps would define its character and future.

Dilemmas and Decisions

Caught in a vortex of moral and strategic dilemmas, I weighed my words carefully. The room hung on a precipice, with each leader grappling with the imminent threat looming just beyond our borders and the ethical implications of our next steps. Alexis' plea echoed in my ears, her ideals clashing starkly against The Iron Lady's ruthless pragmatism.

I stood, my voice steady but my heart heavy. "We stand here today, not just as leaders but as architects of a new era. If we choose force now, what precedent does it set for our future?

Yet, how do we protect our people without the resources we desperately need?"

I paused, looking around the room. "Perhaps there's a middle ground. Could we not show a force of presence, demonstrate our capabilities without immediate aggression? Make them see us as equals, not invaders or easy targets."

Ruslana nodded slowly, her expression thoughtful. "That's a start. A demonstration, a parade of our combined forces near their borders. Show them strength, but also extend a hand once more. If they still refuse to negotiate, we'll be no worse off than we are now."

The Iron Lady raised an eyebrow, her demeanor unyielding. "And if that fails, we will have shown them our hand, and they will still hold all the resources. It's a risk."

"It is," I conceded. "But it's a calculated risk that keeps us on the moral high ground. We must believe in the power of our ideals, not just our weapons."

The room fell silent, each person processing the proposal. Finally, Ruslana spoke again, her voice carrying a mix of resolve and caution. "Let's plan for both. We'll prepare for a show of strength and reach out once more. If they respond, good. If not, we'll be ready to take the next step together."

Alexis squeezed my hand, a silent thank you for voicing a path that still held onto hope. The meeting adjourned with plans to convene the military council and strategic teams to prepare for all possible outcomes.

As we left the hall, the weight of the impending decisions felt lighter, tempered by a tentative hope that perhaps, just perhaps, diplomacy might prevail.

Decisions Made, Lines Drawn

The room fell silent as The Iron Lady's condition hung in the air, heavy and undeniable. I felt the weight of her gaze, as penetrating and strategic as ever, forcing me into a corner from which there was no straightforward escape. Her proposal was not just a tactical maneuver—it was a personal challenge, a test of my mettle and loyalty.

"Fine," I finally said, my voice more resigned than I intended. "I'll go, but not as your subordinate. I'll be there as an observer, a representative of the Republic, to ensure that any actions taken align with our broader strategic objectives."

The Iron Lady's lips twitched, perhaps the closest she ever came to a smile. "Agreed," she replied crisply. "But make no mistake, you'll be in the thick of it with us. This won't be a spectator sport."

Ruslana gave me a sympathetic look but said nothing. Her silence spoke volumes; she was caught between her role as a leader and her personal convictions, much like I was.

As the meeting adjourned, Alexis approached me, her expression a complex tapestry of worry, anger, and resignation. "Be careful," she said simply, her voice thick with unspoken emotions. "I don't like this, not one bit. But I know why you're doing it."

I nodded, unable to articulate everything churning inside me. The drive to protect, the dread of what lay ahead, and the fear of what I was becoming. The Fuego's remnants whispered in my mind, a constant reminder of the potential darkness within, waiting to be unleashed under pressure.

The next few days were a whirlwind of preparations. Maps, intel briefings, logistics—every detail scrutinized and debated. The Iron Lady was a formidable presence, driving her staff and mine to their limits to ensure everything was prepared to perfection.

As we set out for the campaign, I looked back at Farmbridge, its silhouette bathed in the soft light of dusk. It had become more than just a place; it was a symbol of hope, of what we were all fighting to preserve. I carried that image with me as we crossed into no man's land, the boundary between civilization and the wild chaos that awaited us eastward.

The journey was tense, each mile taking us further from home and deeper into uncertainty. I knew that every step was a step towards potential disaster, but turning back wasn't an option. Not anymore. With each passing day, the lines between friend and foe, right and wrong, seemed to blur a little more. I clung to my ideals, but the reality of war was a harsh teacher, and I was its reluctant student.

Tensions Rise and Departures Imminent

As we prepared to leave, the atmosphere was thick with a mix of determination and dread. Alexis, Lilith, Annie, and Wilson were all adamant about not staying behind, their resolve a testament to the bonds we'd forged in adversity. Despite my fears for their safety, I knew their skills would be invaluable on the mission ahead.

"The Iron Lady believes this will be a straightforward raid, but we all know better," I told them during our final briefing. The map on the table was marked with our route and potential hot spots where resistance was expected. "We're not just going to secure supplies; we're walking into a potential hornet's nest."

Annie looked over the map, her finger tracing the paths we planned to take. "We've got your back," she assured me, her voice steady. Lilith nodded in agreement, her usual playful demeanor replaced by a grim seriousness.

Wilson, always the strategist, pointed out alternative routes and backup plans. "If things go sideways, we need to be ready to adapt. Flexibility could make the difference between success and disaster."

The conversation then turned to logistics—ammunition counts, medical supplies, and communication protocols. Every detail was scrutinized, every contingency plan outlined. This wasn't just about fighting; it was about surviving and ensuring we could return to Farm Bridge.

As night fell, I found myself alone with Alexis for a few moments outside. The stars were barely visible through the haze that perpetually shrouded the sky, a constant reminder of the world's fragility.

"I hate that you're caught up in this," I said, my voice barely above a whisper. Alexis reached out, taking my hand in hers, squeezing it tightly.

"We do what we must," she replied. "Just... come back to us. All of you."

Her words hung in the air as we stood in silence, the weight of what lay ahead pressing down on us. The mission would test us all, and I couldn't shake the feeling that not everyone would make it back.

The following morning, we loaded up the vehicles, checked our gear, and said our goodbyes. The Iron Lady was already at the convoy's lead vehicle, her expression unreadable. She gave me a nod as I approached, a silent acknowledgment of the challenges we were about to face together.

"Let's move out," she commanded, her voice cutting through the morning chill. The engines roared to life, and the convoy began to roll out, heading towards uncertainty. As Farm Bridge disappeared behind us, I steeled myself for what was to come, the faces of my friends and the hope of a better future driving me forward.

Wedding Bells Amidst Chaos

Despite the world having turned upside down, the concept of a wedding brought a semblance of normalcy that was refreshing. The entire camp was abuzz with preparations. Everyone chipped in, crafting decorations from salvaged materials and setting up what we hoped would be a picturesque venue in the middle of nowhere.

Lilith had taken charge, her enthusiasm infectious. "We're going to make it beautiful," she declared, organizing teams for various tasks. Flowers were scarce, but she managed to scrounge up enough wildflowers to create a modest bouquet and some decorations.

Annie and Alexis teamed up to prepare the food, managing to put together a feast from our limited supplies. They baked a small cake, a luxury given our circumstances. The mix was rationed flour and powdered eggs, but to us, it was as grand as any wedding cake.

The day of the wedding arrived quicker than expected. Watson, dressed in the cleanest shirt we could find, stood nervously beside Lilith at an improvised altar. Clara, radiant in a dress that had been patched together from various pieces of cloth, walked down the 'aisle'—a path cleared between rows of seated onlookers.

I officiated the ceremony, having been chosen by Watson and Clara for my ability to speak at length when needed. As I spoke about the bonds of love and commitment, I couldn't help but feel a wave of emotion. This was more than just a wedding; it was a statement that despite the apocalypse, we could still find reasons to celebrate, to love, and to hope.

When I pronounced them husband and wife, the cheer that erupted from the crowd was unlike any battle cry or victory shout—it was pure, unadulterated joy. The party that followed was full of laughter, dancing, and, for a few hours, a complete forgetfulness of the harsh world outside.

As the night drew to a close, Watson and Clara thanked everyone. Watson, who had barely said a word throughout his own wedding, managed a heartfelt, "Thank you for reminding us what we're fighting for."

Those words stuck with me as we cleaned up. In the midst of chaos, we had carved out a piece of peace and happiness. It was a reminder of what life could be, of what we all hoped it would return to someday.

Joy Amidst Ruins: A Double Wedding Celebration

The double wedding turned into the biggest event our community had seen since the fall. Without traditional wedding attire or rings, we relied on creativity and solidarity to mark the occasion.

Lilith, bursting with energy, managed the proceedings with an enthusiasm that filled the air with excitement. She had organized a small orchestra of sorts—survivors who could play instruments had been practicing for weeks. The music they produced was uneven but spirited, bringing smiles and tapping feet all around.

Annie and Watson, both notoriously private individuals, found themselves swept up in the festivities despite their reservations. Annie, who had always shied away from the spotlight, blushed deeply but smiled genuinely as she exchanged makeshift vows with Lilith. Watson, for his part, showed a softer side as he looked at Clara, his expression one of deep affection and gratitude.

The feast was a potluck of sorts, with everyone contributing what they could. It was a modest spread by old world standards but a feast by our current ones. People brought out hidden reserves of canned goods, homemade bread, and even a few bottles of pre-war wine someone had been saving for just such an occasion.

As the night drew on, the community danced under the stars. Even Annie and Watson found themselves reluctantly swayed into a slow dance, surrounded by cheering friends. Lilith, of course, was in her element, dancing with anyone and everyone, her laughter ringing out into the night.

It was more than a celebration of two unions; it was a reaffirmation of our community's resilience and a testament to our ability to find happiness in the bleakest of times. As the night wound down, I found myself reflecting on the power of human connection and the enduring strength of hope. We had lost much, but here, in this moment, surrounded by laughter and love, it felt like we could face anything together.

It was time for departure. A detachment from The Iron Lady's forces was scheduled to meet us just north of the devastated Las Vegas. Our journey would start in trucks provided by the Republic, escorting us to the boundary of our territory. From there, we would proceed on foot, integrating with The Iron Lady's troops for a coordinated push northward.

The trucks were packed, and everyone was getting ready for the journey. Watson, Lilith, Annie, and Alexis climbed aboard one of the trucks, their faces a mix of determination and anxiety. Lucky, my faithful companion, looked up at me with his big, pleading eyes. I knelt down to pat his head. "Sorry, buddy, not this time. I'll be back," I assured him, though the promise felt heavy in my heart.

Turning to Robbie and Meg, I gave them a firm hug, the kind that tried to impart every bit of strength and reassurance I could muster. "If we don't come back, you both take Lucky and head north, understand?" Robbie nodded, his expression solemn.

With my rifle slung over my shoulder and a backpack filled with necessary supplies, I made my way to the trucks. The engines were starting up, filling the air with a low rumble that spoke of the imminent dangers and the rough road ahead.

"Hey, wait!" Alexis called out. I turned around to see her jogging towards me, a small, determined look on her face. She reached me, took my hand, and squeezed it tightly. Her touch was grounding, a reminder of what we were fighting to protect.

As we loaded up and the trucks began to roll out, I took one last look back at Farmbridge, the place that had become a symbol of hope and resistance. The journey ahead was fraught with uncertainty, but it was a path we had to take, not just for ourselves but for the future we were trying to build.

Journey Through the Wasteland

Days 846 to 850: The journey along Highway 15 was grim, a stark reminder of the world we now inhabited. As we followed the long stretch leading straight to the ruins of Las Vegas, the landscape around us bore the scars of catastrophe. Burned-out vehicles littered the road, left as haunting monuments to the day the world changed forever.

Our convoy moved cautiously, alert to any dangers that might lurk within the desolate stretches of road that lay outside The Iron Lady's strict jurisdiction. Although her patrols were known to sweep the area regularly, enforcing her severe rules and quashing any signs of dissent or rivalry, the highway remained a no-man's land, a corridor of uncertainty between what was known and the unknown dangers ahead.

As we progressed, the reality of our mission weighed heavily on me. We were marching towards a potential conflict with a group of people who were simply trying to survive, much like ourselves. They held resources critical for our survival against common threats, yet their unwillingness to part with these supplies without conflict put us at an impasse.

Each mile we covered was a mile further into a moral gray area. The trucks rumbled on, each vibration a grim reminder of the inevitable confrontation awaiting us. Our purpose was clear, but the righteousness of our cause felt increasingly tainted by the reality of what we were about to do. We were not just fighting for survival now; we were also struggling with the ethical implications of our actions in a world where right and wrong were no longer easily distinguishable.

Days 851-856: As we descended the rugged terrain of the San Bernardino Mountains, the remnants of past communities haunted our path. The skeletal remains of towns, their inhabitants long dead from the aftermath of nuclear fallout, served as grim milestones.

On one chilly evening, as I tended a small fire, The Iron Lady approached and gestured towards an empty seat next to me. Despite my reluctance, I nodded for her to join. Alexis, Annie, and Lilith were nearby, making use of a spring deemed safe by the readings on a Geiger counter. It was one of the many new normals in our post-apocalyptic world.

We sat in silence, the only sound the crackling of the fire as Evan helped stir the flames. Eventually, she broke the silence, her voice cutting through the crackle of the firewood. "How's your back?" she inquired. Her question brought a rush of discomfort, not from pain, but from the memory of the punishment she had inflicted upon me for defying her in battle. Despite having saved lives, including hers, my disobedience had challenged her authority—a dangerous precedent in a regime built on strict control and unquestionable leadership.

"It's fine," I responded shortly, shifting slightly to ease the stiffness that her mention had brought to mind. The fire popped, sending a small cascade of sparks into the cool night air, mirroring the tension between us.

Evan stared into the flames, her expression unreadable. "When you lead what I lead, you learn quickly that the line between control and chaos is perilously thin. Every decision, every order has weight. Missteps can't be afforded, not when so much is at stake," she said, her tone more reflective than accusatory.

I nodded, understanding her point but not fully agreeing with it. The world had changed, and yet, here we were, repeating the old world's mistakes—fighting over resources, asserting dominance, justifying harsh actions under the guise of necessity. The fire crackled between us, a barrier of warmth in the cold reality of our circumstances.

Reflections by the Firelight

Days 851-856: As we continued our solemn vigil by the fire, The Iron Lady shared her thoughts, a rare glimpse into her world-weary soul. She spoke of the chaos that reigned before her rise to power, the anarchic landscape that had sprawled endlessly across what was once America. Her words painted a picture of a land torn by factions, where survival was the only law and human life was as cheap as the ammunition that claimed it.

"I gave them a purpose," she stated, her eyes reflecting the flickering flames, revealing a flicker of vulnerability. "It wasn't easy, and it sure as hell wasn't pretty. A lot of people died. But then, they would have died anyway. The difference is, I built something. Not just survival, but a civilization. From the bloodshed, I crafted order."

She paused, her gaze lost in the dance of the fire. "I wonder sometimes... did I save more than I killed?" Her voice was almost a whisper, laden with the weight of her actions.

"You said it yourself, Evan," I responded, hoping to offer some solace in the harsh truth she faced. "People would have died either way."

She nodded, a thoughtful look etching her features. "I knew

you'd see it my way," she murmured. "Remember what it took to unite these groups. And remember what will happen if there's no one strong enough to hold the reins."

Her last words hung in the air, heavy with foreboding. "What's coming... no one will be the same after it. And some of us might not make it."

As Lilith and Alexis's voices approached, signaling a return to the reality waiting beyond our small circle of light, Evan stood, replacing her cap and resettling the mask of leadership upon her visage. She stepped away from the fire, the brief moment of vulnerability shielded once again behind a facade of unyielding strength.

Days 869-872: The stillness of the night was shattered by a sharp cry—a warning cut short by a deadly silence that followed. We were under attack. The initial arrow that struck our sentry was not perfectly aimed, but it was effective enough to silence him after a brief, gurgling cry. That cry was enough; it had done its job. We were alerted, and immediately, the camp sprung into action.

The Fuego within me surged to the forefront, fueling a response that was both raw, unbridled fury and chillingly precise execution. I moved through the shadows, my body reacting with a predator's instinct, guided by the flickering fires and moonlight that cast long shadows around our encampment.

Armed with nothing more than my rifle and the lingering adrenaline of past battles, I navigated through the underbrush, circling around the source of the attack. The attackers were likely not expecting such swift and fierce retaliation. Their initial advantage of surprise was quickly neutralized as I closed in on their position.

As I approached, the rustling of leaves and the soft murmurs of their communication guided me to their hideout. They were a small band, likely scouts from a rival group, emboldened by the darkness. With each step closer, my training and the drug's influence intermingled, turning every sense up to an excruciating sharpness.

Without hesitation, I engaged. The firefight was brutal and brief. Each shot from my rifle was aimed with lethal precision, dictated by a mind that operated on the brink of frenzy yet controlled by years of disciplined training. The attackers, caught off-guard by the ferocity and speed of my assault, were quickly overwhelmed.

In the aftermath, as the adrenaline slowly ebbed away, replaced by the heavy, cold realization of what had just transpired, I stood among the fallen enemies. The night air was thick with the scent of gunpowder and blood, a stark reminder of the dark path we were on.

As I returned to the camp, the faces of my companions mirrored the horror and relief that such nights brought us. We were alive, but at what cost? The darkness of the night seemed to deepen, holding within it the echoes of the violence that had just unfolded.

Days 869-872: In the eerie quiet that followed the confrontation, I stood alone among the trees, the darkness around me seeming to pulse with the aftermath of violence. The last of the attackers lay at my feet, his eyes wide open in a silent, eternal stare. The fight had ended as swiftly as it had begun, but the silence was heavy, laden with the weight of what had transpired

I returned to the camp, moving through the shadows, my side throbbing dully with each step. It was only as I emerged into the dim light cast by the dying fires that I realized the extent of my injury. A deep gash across my ribs—painful but not life-threatening. I pressed a hand against the wound, feeling the warm blood that seeped through my fingers. It was a stark reminder of the night's brutal reality.

As I approached the camp, the faces of my companions came into view, etched with relief and fear. They had gathered around the fires, their weapons still in hand, eyes darting into the darkness beyond the camp's fragile perimeter. The air was thick with the smell of gunpowder and blood, a tangible reminder of the death that had come so close.

Alexis was among them, her face a mixture of relief and horror as she saw me. Her eyes fell on the blood-soaked side of my shirt, and she rushed over, her hands reaching out to steady me as I swayed slightly.

"We need to get you patched up," she said urgently, her voice a low whisper that barely rose above the crackling of the fire.

I nodded, allowing her to lead me to where a small medical kit lay open, its contents hastily scrambled. As she cleaned the wound, her hands were steady, but I could feel the tension in her every touch.

"Why didn't you call out? We could have helped," she murmured as she worked.

I didn't answer immediately. The truth was, the Fuego had driven me to act alone, to revel in the visceral satisfaction of the hunt. It was a part of me that I feared, a darkness that was all-consuming.

"I had to," I finally said, my voice low. "It was safer this way."

She didn't press further, but I saw the worry deepen in her eyes. It was a look I had seen too often, a fear not just for my physical safety, but for the part of me that might be lost to Fuego's savage call.

The rest of the night passed in a tense vigilance. We reset our watches, fortified our position, and tended to the wounded. As dawn broke over the camp, the light revealed the true cost of the night. Blood stained the ground, and the air held a chill that went beyond the early morning cold.

We were alive, but each encounter with death left its mark on us, a reminder of the fragile thread that held us to this life. As we prepared to move out, I felt the weight of every life I had taken, a burden I carried deep inside, alongside the burning embers of the Fuego.

Days 875 to 879: As we continued our journey, the landscape around us gradually changed. The desolation of the scorched earth gave way to sparse patches of vegetation—a sign of life persevering in the face of adversity. The group's mood lifted slightly with the scenery, a welcome distraction from the recent violence.

Each evening, as we made camp, Alexis would quietly tend to my wound, her touch gentle yet firm, her presence a constant reminder of the life I fought to return to. Though the physical scars were healing, the mental ones lingered, a silent testament to the battles fought both externally and within.

One night, under the clear skies finally free of the oppressive smoke that had blanketed them for so long, I found myself unable to sleep. The fire crackled softly in the background, its glow a small beacon in the darkness. Alexis sat beside me, her hand finding mine in the dim light.

"You've been quiet," she murmured, squeezing my hand. "Talk to me."

I hesitated, the words caught in my throat. How could I explain the darkness that the Fuego had awakened? How could I confess that part of me had thrived on the chaos and violence it demanded?

"It's hard," I finally said, my voice barely above a whisper. "Back there, in the arena, I felt... powerful. In control. But it was an illusion. The Fuego... it takes more than it gives."

Alexis nodded, her eyes reflecting the firelight. "I can't pretend to understand what that's like. But I know you. The man you are, the one you strive to be—that's who you really are, not what the drug makes you feel."

Her words were a balm to the turmoil inside me. "I'm trying, Lex. Every day, it's a fight."

"I know," she replied softly. "And you don't have to fight it alone."

We sat in silence for a while, watching the stars. It was moments like these that reminded me of what was at stake, of what we were fighting for—not just survival, but the chance to reclaim a life worth living.

As we broke camp the next morning, the mood was somber yet determined. We knew the challenges ahead would be formidable, but together, we held on to the hope that at the end of this journey, peace might finally greet us. With each step forward, we carried not just the weight of our past but the promise of our future.

Strategic Maneuvers and Arrival at Indian Springs

Days 880-885: As we navigated north towards Pahrump, avoiding the still-dangerous remnants of Las Vegas, our convoy was met by riders bearing the emblem of the Army of the Dawn. Their sudden appearance initially sent a ripple of tension through our ranks, but The Iron Lady's calm demeanor quelled any potential conflict. She was familiar with these Scouts, who were part of her intricate network of operatives.

The Scouts were there to escort us via a less traveled, yet quicker route around Mount Charleston. This detour was a welcome shortcut, cutting our travel time significantly and demonstrating The Iron Lady's strategic foresight. The path was rugged, winding through areas that had escaped the worst of the fallout and offered a somewhat safer passage.

Upon reaching the outskirts of Indian Springs, it was clear why this route had been chosen. Positioned strategically, Indian Springs was far enough from the heart of the devastation to remain viable but close enough to be of strategic importance. The town had once been a sleepy settlement but had grown in prominence after the nearby military facilities were abandoned in the chaos following the nuclear strikes.

As we set up a temporary camp just outside the town, The Iron Lady convened a brief meeting with her Scouts and our group's leaders. The air was thick with anticipation and the weight of the impending operations. There was a sense that what we did next could significantly alter the balance of power in the region.

Evan's planning was evident in every detail, from the allocation of resources to the timing of our movements. Despite my misgivings about her methods, it was impossible not to respect her ability to orchestrate complex operations under such dire circumstances.

Our objective was clear: secure the military stockpile in Indian Springs and ensure it could be used to bolster the defenses against the encroaching threats. With the Scouts' local knowledge and our combined forces, we were better positioned than I had hoped. Yet, as we prepared for the next phase of our mission, I couldn't shake the feeling that each step forward was also a step deeper into a moral quagmire from which there might be no return.

Days 890-891: As we descended the final stretches of the mountain terrain and approached the open desert, the sight that greeted us was far from reassuring. Instead of the organized military presence we expected near Indian Springs, ominous plumes of smoke rose in the distance, indicating trouble. The absence of the Army of the Dawn's forces was alarming, and the air was thick with the smell of recent conflict.

Evan, as ever composed, brushed aside my concerns with a brisk command to continue moving forward. Her assurance that everything was under control did little to ease the growing sense of dread among us. Alexis's distrust of Evan was palpable; she watched her with a mix of resentment and wariness, clearly skeptical of the situation unfolding before us.

Annie, typically stoic, kept her composure but was visibly on edge. Her readiness to react at a moment's notice, with her hand close to her weapon, spoke volumes about her apprehension. In contrast, Lilith expressed her anxiety openly, frequently voicing her concerns and questioning Evan's lack of communication about our next steps.

As we moved closer to the source of the smoke, the silence of the desert was unnerving. The usual signs of military operation —radio chatter, vehicle movements, the hustle of troops— were conspicuously absent. This eerie quietude, combined with the visible signs of destruction, suggested that something significant and potentially disastrous had occurred.

The tension within our group escalated with each step closer to Indian Springs. It was clear that we were walking into a situation that might require us to switch from a strategic mission to survival mode at any moment. The uncertainty of not knowing what lay ahead, coupled with Evan's cryptic assurances, left us all on high alert, prepared for any eventuality as we continued our cautious advance toward the smoking remnants of what was supposed to be our rendezvous point.

Days 892 to 895: As we arrived at Indian Springs, the devastation was palpable. Bodies of the fallen had been hastily dealt with; the soldiers of the Army of the Dawn received funeral pyres, a mark of respect in the midst of chaos, while the local settlers, less fortunate, were unceremoniously dumped into a massive, open grave.

The battle that had taken place here was not just a tactical engagement but a brutal massacre. The Iron Lady had exploited the fanaticism growing within her ranks, a dark and growing cult of personality that worshiped her as a deity. She had sent her own fanatical troops, disguised as negotiators, who detonated themselves amidst the settler leaders, effectively decapitating the local resistance in a single, horrifying strike.

This ruthless tactic threw the settlers into chaos. Well-armed and desperate, they fought back with everything they had, utilizing mortars and heavy artillery that they had presumably stockpiled for such an eventuality. The landscape around us bore the scars of this fierce resistance, with craters and burned-out buildings painting a grim picture of the last stand that took place here.

Evan's reaction to the use of suicide bombers was chillingly pragmatic. She regarded these sacrificial soldiers as merely another tool to achieve her objectives. This cold utilitarianism was both horrifying and morbidly fascinating—a reflection of the lengths she was willing to go to maintain control and achieve victory.

As we walked through the aftermath, the air was heavy with the acrid smell of smoke and death. The silence that hung over the area was a stark reminder of the cost of this conflict. Not just in lives, but in the erosion of any moral high ground we might have once claimed. The settlers' desperate defense and their ultimate defeat were a brutal testament to the harsh realities of war in this new world order.

Each step we took through Indian Springs was a step through a graveyard of not just bodies but of principles, where the lines between right and wrong blurred into obscurity under the harsh desert sun.

Reflections at Indian Springs

Days 896 to 897: The Iron Lady had deliberately brought us to Indian Springs not just as spectators but as witnesses to the harsh realities of her methods. She wanted us to understand the brutal cost of victory, to see firsthand the sacrifices required to secure stability and power in this lawless new world. Her philosophy was simple yet chilling: to win at all costs and maintain control, no matter the human toll.

As we stood in one of the large hangars, once bustling with the activity of the U.S. Air Force but now repurposed as a depot for the spoils of war, I saw the fruits of her victory. The hangar was filled not just with military hardware but also with people—the survivors of the battle who were now prisoners. Those who were healthy enough were earmarked for slavery; the others were left to a fate too grim to contemplate.

Alexis and Lilith could not stand the sight. The blatant disregard for human life, the commodification of people as mere resources to be used, consumed, or discarded—it was too much. Hatred, pure and unyielding, had finally found its way into Alexis's eyes. She had to walk away, the burden of the scene too heavy to bear in silence. Annie, ever the stoic, allowed herself a rare moment of visible distress. The implications of what had occurred here, the stripping of humanity from individuals who had fought desperately for their survival, were clear and profoundly disturbing.

Evan's explanation to me was a cold reminder of her worldview. "I wanted you to see the cost of victory," she had said, as if the scorched earth and shattered lives were necessary evils, unavoidable in the pursuit of greater security and order. But standing there, amidst the spoils of war and the broken survivors, it became clear that the line between necessary evil and moral bankruptcy was perilously thin.

This wasn't just a battle; it was a statement of intent from The Iron Lady—a demonstration of her willingness to go to any lengths to secure her objectives. But as I looked around at the consequences of such a philosophy, I wondered at what point the cost becomes too great. At what point do we lose ourselves in the pursuit of what we claim to protect? The silence that filled the hangar was not just a pause between conversations; it was a quiet reflection on the path we had taken, a path that seemed increasingly difficult to justify.

Days 898 to 899: Alexis was overwhelmed by the horrors we had witnessed at Indian Springs. As she cried in my arms, the weight of our actions and the reality of our choices sunk in deeply. The pain and frustration she felt were a stark reminder of the moral costs associated with the path we had chosen to walk alongside The Iron Lady.

The Iron Lady's methods, while effective in achieving military and strategic objectives, had left a trail of human suffering that was hard to reconcile with any notion of a better future. Her belief that strength and control were paramount to rebuilding civilization had led to decisions that prioritized power over compassion, and efficiency over ethics.

In her eyes, the harsh actions taken were necessary evils—steps towards stabilizing a chaotic world. But as I held Alexis, feeling her sorrow and despair, I couldn't help but question the true cost of such a philosophy. How many lives were shattered, how many spirits broken to secure a moment of peace or a strategic advantage?

The conversation with The Iron Lady echoed in my mind. She had acknowledged the potential backlash, the hatred that her actions might breed. Yet, she remained steadfast in her belief that strength and dominance were essential to maintain order and build a new world. This utilitarian approach, stripping away the individual suffering involved, seemed increasingly flawed as I considered the faces of those we had hurt, directly or indirectly.

These moments of reflection were crucial. They were a reminder that the path to rebuilding wasn't just about securing resources or defeating enemies; it was about the values we chose to uphold in the process. If we continued down a path where the ends always justifies the means, what kind of society would we end up creating? Could a truly just and sustainable civilization arise from the ashes of such ruthless tactics?

As the night wore on, the burden of these thoughts grew heavier. Alexis's tears were not just for the victims at Indian Springs, but for all of us, caught in a cycle of violence and retribution that seemed destined to repeat itself unless we found a new way forward.

Return of the Air Force

Days 900 to 901: The roar of engines filled the air as the convoy prepared to depart, laden with munitions and supplies for the forthcoming battles. Amidst this noise, the distinctive sound of an aircraft penetrated the cacophony, drawing all eyes upwards. A C-27 cargo plane, unmistakable with its broad wings and the logo of the United States Air Force emblazoned on its sides, cut through the clouds and flew directly overhead.

The sight was startling and unexpected, a stark reminder of the world beyond our immediate conflicts. The plane's presence suggested that there were still operational elements of the U.S. military active, perhaps monitoring the situation or even preparing to intervene. This revelation brought a mix of hope and anxiety.

As the plane passed, it dropped several small packages by parachute, which fluttered down towards our location. The packages landed scattered around the edges of our convoy, prompting a rush to retrieve them. Inside, we found not only medical supplies but also communication equipment and maps. The most significant item, however, was a radio set to a specific frequency, along with a note urging us to establish contact.

The sudden provision of aid and the call to communicate were a clear indication that the U.S. government, or what remained of it, was not only aware of our struggles but was also reaching out to assist. This development could potentially change the dynamics of our current engagements. The possibility of coordinating with what remained of national military forces offered a new strategic advantage, but it also raised questions about their intentions and the broader geopolitical landscape we were about to re-enter.

We gathered around the radio, tuning it to the specified frequency. After a few moments of static, a clear voice broke through, identifying themselves as part of a U.S. military command center monitoring the region. They requested a sitrep (situation report), signaling the beginning of what could be a significant shift in our local power structures and our fight against the Aztecos and other threats.

This unexpected lifeline from the sky prompted a quick huddle among our leaders. Decisions needed to be made about how to engage with this newfound ally. The strategic implications were immense; aligning with U.S. military forces could provide the support we desperately needed to tip the scales in our favor. However, it also meant navigating a new set of alliances and potentially exposing ourselves to unknown agendas.

As we debated our next steps, the reality of our situation became clearer. We were no longer isolated players in a post-apocalyptic theater; we were part of a larger narrative unfolding across the remnants of the United States. The war was evolving, and with this new connection, so too would our strategies and objectives. The road ahead was uncertain, but for the first time in a long while, it seemed there might be a path forward that could lead us out of perpetual conflict and towards something resembling peace.

As we journeyed back to Farmbridge, the hum of the engine underlined our collective silence. Each of us lost in our own thoughts, grappling with the weight of recent events—the leaflet I held was a tangible symbol of a world struggling to right itself after teetering on the brink of total collapse.

Alexis sat beside me, her gaze fixed on the passing landscape, but I knew her mind was miles away, replaying the horrors we had witnessed at Indian Springs. The reality of what had transpired there, fueled by decisions made under the guise of necessity, hung heavily between us. It was a stark reminder of how easily the line between right and wrong could blur in times of war.

The leaflet's message, "You are not forgotten. You were not abandoned. America remains," felt like a lifeline but also a sobering reminder of how isolated we had become. The promise of a speech from the president was a beacon of hope, a signal that perhaps there was a chance to rebuild not just our lives but the very fabric of our nation.

As we neared Farmbridge, the radio crackled to life, breaking the silence that had enveloped the truck. We listened intently as the broadcaster reiterated the upcoming presidential address. The specified AM frequencies were listed again, a call to tune in and hear from a leader many had presumed dead or incapacitated.

The weight of the flyer in my hand seemed to grow heavier with each mile. It represented so much more than just a piece of paper; it was a testament to the resilience of a nation and the enduring spirit of its people. Yet, it also posed new questions and uncertainties about the future. What had the U.S. government been doing all this time? What could the president possibly say to a nation shattered by nuclear war and fractured by internal strife?

As we pulled into Farmbridge, the familiar sights did little to ease the sense of foreboding that had settled over me. I knew that the upcoming broadcast would be a pivotal moment not just for the remnants of the United States but for each of us personally. How we responded to the president's words could well determine the path forward for our fledgling republic and for each of us as individuals still fighting for a semblance of peace in a ravaged world.

The truck stopped, and we disembarked, each of us carrying the weight of our experiences and the faint stirrings of hope kindled by the promise of a reunited America. As we gathered together, waiting for the next day's broadcast, I looked around at the faces of my companions, marked by the trials of survival but also by a resilient determination to forge a better future. In that moment, despite everything, I felt a profound connection to the larger tapestry of human endurance and the unyielding desire to reclaim our place in a world we still called home.

Presidential Address in Farmbridge

As the sun began its descent over Farmbridge, the remnants of the community gathered around makeshift speakers, all eyes fixed on the radio. The static crackled to life, and the President of the United States began to speak, his voice resonant yet carrying an unmistakable burden.

"Today, I speak to you not just as your President, but as a fellow survivor of the greatest catastrophe our nation has ever faced. Over these past three years, our country has been tested in ways we never imagined. But despite the darkness that has fallen over our land, today, I am here to tell you that hope is not lost."

The crowd listened intently, hanging on every word, as the President outlined the efforts of what remained of the U.S. government. He spoke of hidden bases and contingencies, of brave men and women fighting to keep the idea of America alive.

"We have faced unimaginable challenges," he continued, "from the devastation of nuclear strikes to the breakdown of our most basic societal structures. Yet, through it all, we have maintained pockets of resistance and resilience. Our military forces, though scattered, remain active. Our government, though beleaguered, continues to function."

The President then addressed the recovery efforts, detailing plans to reconnect isolated communities, rebuild infrastructure, and restore law and order. He spoke of forming new alliances and rebuilding the nation from the ground up.

"But we cannot do this alone," he asserted. "In the coming days, we will be reaching out to community leaders across the former United States. We will need your cooperation and your strength. Together, we can rebuild our nation, and ensure that the values upon which it was founded are preserved for future generations."

As the broadcast concluded, a murmur of discussion broke out among the listeners. The message had been one of hope, but also of immense responsibility. It was clear that the road ahead would be fraught with challenges, but for the first time in years, there seemed to be a definitive plan and a guiding hand at the helm.

Back at Farmbridge, as the crowd dispersed, I found myself reflecting on the President's words. They had stirred something within me—a sense of duty, perhaps, or a renewed sense of purpose. The idea that America could rise again from its ashes was daunting, yet it was a challenge I felt compelled to meet head-on.

The conversation turned to plans for the future. Ruslana, now more than ever, seemed determined to ensure that Farmbridge played a pivotal role in the reformation of the country. The community, though wary, was invigorated by the prospect of being part of something larger than themselves.

As night fell over Farmbridge, I felt a cautious optimism. The President's address had reminded us all that while the path forward was uncertain, it was not uncharted. We had survived the worst; now it was time to work towards a better future, not just for ourselves, but for all who would come after us.

Rebuilding America

The community of Farmbridge gathered once more as the remnants of the broadcast echoed through the makeshift speakers, leaving a solemn yet hopeful silence in its wake. The President's voice, resonant despite the static, had spoken of peace and the Herculean task of rebuilding a nation from its scattered ashes.

"An unconditional peace has been reached," the President had declared, marking the end of a conflict that had left no victors, only survivors. His words, though grave, carried a promise—that from the ruins of old conflicts and the current devastation, America would rise once more.

"In the days ahead, the task will be monumental," the President continued. "Our forces abroad are returning, and our Navy remains a beacon of hope and capability. We will reach out, reconnect, and rebuild. Every survivor settlement from east to west is a cornerstone on which we will rebuild the United States."

The mention of reconnaissance and damage assessment teams stirred a mix of anxiety and anticipation among the people of Farmbridge. The promise of federal assistance was a lifeline, a sign that their struggles were recognized and that help was on its way.

"I ask for your cooperation," the President implored. "Welcome these teams. Assist them. Together, we will assess the damage, catalog our needs, and begin the arduous process of reconstruction. It won't be easy. The nights may be long, but there is a new dawn on the horizon."

As the broadcast concluded, the community leaders, including Ruslana, began to discuss what the President's words meant for them. It was clear that the path forward would require collaboration, not just within Farmbridge but with neighboring settlements and the federal teams that would soon arrive.

"Preparations must begin immediately," Ruslana announced, addressing the crowd. "We need to organize, to catalog our resources, our needs, and our capabilities. When the federal teams arrive, we must be ready to show them that Farmbridge is more than a survivor settlement—it is a vital part of the new America."

The tasks ahead were daunting. Infrastructure needed rebuilding, supplies needed organizing, and defenses needed fortifying. Yet, there was now a blueprint, a directive from the highest level of what remained of the federal government.

As the meeting dispersed, the residents of Farmbridge felt a renewed sense of purpose. The war might be over, and the peace might be fragile, but the rebuilding of America had just begun. In the days to come, they would work, not just to survive, but to thrive—to ensure that when history looked back on these dark times, it would tell of a community that stood together to bring about a new dawn for their nation.

As the night deepened, the debate within the Farmbridge community grew more heated. The President's message had sparked a wildfire of hope and skepticism in equal measure. Some clung to the promise of a reborn America, while others scoffed at the notion, seeing it as a distant dream, irrelevant to their immediate struggles.

I slipped away from the crowd, feeling the burden of the Fuego burning within me. The promise of peace and rebuilding seemed almost alien compared to the relentless fight for survival that had defined our lives for so long.

Alone, I walked towards the outskirts of Farmbridge, where the stark reality of our existence stood in sharp contrast to the hopeful words from the broadcast. Here, the remnants of war were evident—buildings still scarred by fire, streets littered with the detritus of a society that had once thrived.

The conversation behind me faded into a background murmur, and I focused on the tangible things: the cool night air, the uneven ground under my feet, and the ever-present ache in my ribs where Fuego's fury had left its mark.

"The president might be sincere," I muttered to myself, "but what can he really offer us now?" The infrastructure to support a nationwide recovery was in shambles. The logistics alone were a nightmare to consider. How long would it take for help to actually reach places like Farmbridge?

And then there was the Iron Lady, a reminder of the harsh realities of power and control. Her empire, built on the backs of the desperate and the ruthless, wouldn't easily relinquish its hold, peace or no peace.

As I walked, I pondered the challenges ahead. Would we really be able to integrate back into an America governed from afar, or had we become too detached, too hardened by our own trials to fit back into the mold of a nation state?

Perhaps more pressingly, I wondered about my own future. Fuego's grip was a sentence that hung over me—a countdown to an inevitable end. No presidential promise could change that reality.

Turning back towards the settlement, I realized that regardless of the broader national picture, our immediate future depended on the choices we made here, in Farmbridge. Would we reach out to embrace the promise of help, or would we continue to rely solely on our own resilience?

As I rejoined the group, still deep in debate, I knew that whatever decision we made, it wouldn't be without its consequences. But for now, at least, we had a choice to make, and that in itself was a kind of freedom that had been in short supply over the last three years.

In the makeshift workshop filled with the scent of sawdust and old wood, Watson worked meticulously on a wooden horse, his way of contributing to a sense of normalcy in our increasingly militarized community. He looked up from his project, meeting my gaze with a knowing look.

"Yeah, I feel it," he admitted, setting down his tools.

"Everything's moving too fast. We're gearing up for a fight none of us really understand. Not against the aztecos or any raiders, but against something bigger, something that doesn't fit into the world as we know it anymore."

I nodded, leaning against a workbench cluttered with various woodworking tools. The community was buzzing outside, a mixture of fear and anticipation hanging in the air as preparations for the impending conflict continued.

"It's like we're pawns in a much larger game now," I continued, watching Watson pick up the wooden horse and examine it. "With the president's speech and all the military movements, it feels like we're just pieces being moved around by people who haven't lived a day in our reality."

Watson grunted in agreement, his fingers tracing the smooth curves of the wooden horse. "Exactly. We're supposed to be part of this great rebuilding, but at what cost? We're trading one form of chaos for another, hoping it turns out better this time around."

The sound of machinery and orders shouted in the distance filtered through the workshop walls. Outside, soldiers practiced drills while others loaded supplies into trucks and armored vehicles.

"And what about us, the people here, in Farmbridge?" I asked, gesturing toward the window where a group of children were watching the soldiers with a mix of awe and confusion. "What happens to our plans for peace and rebuilding our own lives when we're drawn into a conflict that might not even be ours to fight?"

Watson put down the horse and wiped his hands on a cloth.

"That's the million-dollar question, isn't it? We sign up to fight someone else's war, and we risk losing everything we've worked so hard to protect here. Or we sit back and hope that someone else's decisions don't lead to our downfall."

He stood and walked over to the doorway, looking out over the bustling community. "I guess all we can do is prepare the best we can, teach these young soldiers how to survive, not just how to fight."

I followed him to the door, watching as Alana ran past, chasing a makeshift ball with other children. Her laughter was a brief respite from the weight of our conversation.

"We'll keep training, keep preparing," Watson said as he turned back to me. "But keep one eye open, always. We're not just fighting for survival anymore. We're fighting for the right to define what comes next. And I don't know about you, but I'm not ready to give up that right just yet."

As Watson returned to his workbench, I left the workshop, my thoughts heavy with the complexities of our situation. The balance between fighting for survival and fighting for the future was delicate, and every step we took now could tip the scales in ways we might not be ready to handle.

Doubts and Strategies

In the quiet workshop, Watson and I settled into a deeper discussion about the situation. The hum of activity outside seemed distant as we focused on the troubling thoughts at hand.

"You're right, Watson. The Iron Lady's losses seem out of proportion, even considering the aztecos' ferocity," I said, watching him apply a final coat of varnish to the wooden horse.

"It's almost as if she's losing on purpose, or at least not fighting as hard as she could. Could be a tactic to draw more people under her command, or maybe to push us into a corner where we have no choice but to support her more aggressively."

Watson wiped his hands and leaned back against the workbench, his gaze thoughtful. "Exactly. And if we march right into that trap, we're just fodder. If we're going to support her, we need to do it on our terms. We need eyes on the ground, our own intelligence. Can't rely solely on what she tells us."

The idea of going into a potential conflict with such high stakes without clear, independent information was unnerving. "We should set up our own recon teams," I suggested. "Groups that can move ahead and around the main forces. They need to be small, fast, and capable of blending in. They'd report directly to us, not through the usual channels."

Watson nodded, warming to the strategy. "Good idea. And we keep this close to the chest. The fewer who know, the better. We can pick a few trusted individuals, train them up quick. I know a few folks who would be perfect for this."

The notion of conducting our own operations within the larger movement felt like a step back towards autonomy, something we'd been gradually losing amid the escalating conflict. "This isn't just about gathering intel," I added, "It's about ensuring we're not being manipulated into serving someone else's agenda. We protect our people first and foremost."

"Yeah," Watson agreed, his expression hardening with resolve. "And if it turns out there's treachery afoot, we'll be prepared to take necessary actions. Not just for survival, but to ensure that whatever future we're building isn't corrupted from the start."

As we continued to plan, the weight of leadership felt heavy but clear. Decisions made here could save lives or lead to disaster. The quiet clinking of Watson's tools as he resumed his work underscored the gravity of our conversation. This was about more than just survival now; it was about safeguarding a future that remained uncertain but was worth fighting for.

"We'll start first thing tomorrow," I concluded, standing up to leave. "I'll draft a list of potential candidates for the recon teams and run them by you."

Watson nodded, his focus already shifting back to his work, a symbol of the normalcy we were all fighting to protect. "Alright. Let's do what we must. Just remember, no matter how dark it gets, we're not just fighting for today. We're fighting for the kind of tomorrow we want to wake up to."

Stepping out of the workshop, I felt a renewed sense of purpose. The path forward was fraught with challenges, but with careful planning and a bit of cautious optimism, we could navigate through the storm.

Ruslana stood firm at the firing range, her presence commanding even from a distance. As Robbie and I approached, I could see her instructing a group of civilians, transforming everyday people into capable defenders of their community. It was a sight that filled me with both pride and a pang of solemnity—these were the real stakes of our struggle.

"Ruslana," I greeted her as we came close, noticing her eyes briefly flick to Robbie before returning to me with a steely gaze.

She nodded, her focus shifting back to the group. "Glad you

could join us. We're training more of our people—not just to fight, but to protect themselves. Can't have too many skilled hands."

I watched as a middle-aged woman successfully hit a distant target, a look of surprised pride spreading across her face. Ruslana clapped her on the back, encouraging her. "Good shot, Marlene! Keep it steady now."

Turning back to me, Ruslana's voice lowered so only I could hear. "I wanted to discuss your role in the upcoming operations. The Iron Lady's liaisons are here, as you've seen. They're a necessary evil, but keep your friends close and your enemies closer, right?"

I nodded, understanding the gravity of her strategy. "They're keeping tabs on us, no doubt. We'll do the same."

Ruslana gestured toward the liaisons who were trying to blend in but sticking out like sore thumbs. "Exactly. I trust you've heard they've been asking about you? Seems you've made quite the impression. They call you 'The Scout.' Not just because of your military background, but because you have a knack for seeing things others don't."

I chuckled dryly. "A nickname is the least of my worries. What's the plan for using this newfound reputation?"

She was straightforward, "You're going with them. Not just as a watchful eye, but as our voice. Make sure our interests are protected. And if you see a chance to gather some intel, you take it."

The idea of embedding deeper within the Iron Lady's ranks wasn't appealing, but it made strategic sense. "Understood. I'll keep our bases covered."

"Good," Ruslana said, turning her attention back to the firing range. "Remember, it's not just about shooting a gun. It's about knowing when to pull the trigger and when to hold back. That applies out there too. Be smart about it."

As Robbie and I walked away, he elbowed me jokingly. "Look at you, 'The Scout' heading off on another adventure. Just make sure to come back to us, okay?"

I nodded, feeling the weight of my responsibilities. "I'll do my best, Robbie. That's all I can promise."

The conversation with Ruslana had set things into motion. I was to be a part of the convoy heading east, not just as a participant but as a guardian of our community's future. As the landscape of conflict continued to evolve, so too did my role within it—no longer just a survivor, but a protector, a scout in more ways than one.

Handling Discontent in Farm Bridge

Ruslana carefully wiped down her rifle, her movements methodical and precise. We sat in the quiet of the late afternoon, each of us processing the weight of the situation.

"Alexis has a point, of course," Ruslana finally broke the silence. "What happened at Indian Springs... it's not something we can just brush under the rug. People need to express their concerns, and rightfully so."

I nodded slowly, understanding the delicate balance she was trying to maintain. "I know. And suppressing those voices isn't the answer. But maybe we can channel that energy into something constructive."

Ruslana looked up from her rifle, interested. "What do you suggest?"

"Maybe a forum—a place and time for everyone to voice their concerns openly. Not just about Indian Springs, but about how we move forward. It could help prevent these feelings from boiling over into something uncontrollable."

Ruslana considered this, then nodded. "A forum might work. It gives people a chance to be heard, which might ease some of the tension. Plus, it shows we're not ignoring the problem."

"We should include voices from all the settlements, not just Farm Bridge," I added. "If we're really going to be a Republic, then it needs to be a collective effort."

"Agreed," Ruslana said as she reassembled her rifle with a final click. "I'll organize it. Can I count on you to talk to Alexis? Help her understand that we're trying to do this the right way?"

"I'll talk to her," I promised, though I was unsure how to bridge the gap between her ideals and the harsh realities we faced. "She needs to know she's not alone in her feelings. That might help."

"Good," Ruslana stood, her rifle now pristine. "And let her know about the forum. It might give her a constructive outlet for her frustrations."

As we walked back towards the community center, I felt a mix of apprehension and hope. Handling the discontent brewing in our ranks was crucial, not just for maintaining order but for ensuring our survival in a world that remained unforgiving and chaotic. The upcoming forum wouldn't solve everything, but it was a step in the right direction—a step towards truly building something that could last beyond the conflicts and crises of the present.

Difficult Conversations and Unity

In the soft glow of the bedside lamp, Alexis turned to face me, her expression weary yet resolved. "I know we need unity, especially now. But unity shouldn't come at the cost of our morals, or by silencing voices that challenge us to be better."

I nodded, feeling the weight of her words. "I understand, and I'm not saying you shouldn't speak up. Maybe there's a way to address these issues without dividing everyone. Ruslana is planning a forum where everyone can express their concerns openly. It might help bridge the gap between different viewpoints."

Alexis considered this for a moment, her eyes reflecting a mix of hope and skepticism. "A forum could be good. It's a start, at least. People need to know that their leaders are listening and that they care about more than just survival. They need to know we care about how we survive."

"That's fair," I replied. "And you should be a part of that conversation. Your voice is important, Alexis. You remind us of who we want to be, not just what we have to do to survive."

She smiled faintly, a slight easing of the tension in her shoulders. "Thanks for understanding. I'll speak at the forum. Maybe if we can openly discuss these things, we can find a way forward that doesn't compromise our values."

"I believe we can," I said, squeezing her hand gently. "And

whatever happens, I'm with you. We'll face whatever comes, together."

As we lay back down, I thought about the delicate balance we were trying to maintain. The Republic was still in its infancy, vulnerable and untested. The upcoming forum wasn't just about resolving current issues—it was about setting a precedent for how we would handle challenges in the future. If we could navigate this successfully, perhaps we could truly build something lasting and worthy of the sacrifices so many had made.

As the sun began to set over Farm Bridge, casting long shadows across the newly pitched tents outside the protective walls, the air was filled with a mix of tension and purpose. Soldiers from various settlements had converged here, transforming the once quiet refuge into a bustling military camp. The sight of tents sprawling into the horizon underscored the scale of our upcoming endeavor—a joint operation unlike any other since the catastrophe.

Clay, accompanied by a contingent of combat-hardened veterans, made his way through the camp, greeting old friends and introducing his troops. These men and women, veterans of America's conflicts across the globe, brought not only their experience but also a disciplined calm that was infectious.

I walked alongside Clay, discussing logistics and strategies. "It's good to have you here, Clay. Your team looks solid," I commented, observing the veterans as they efficiently set up their area.

"Yeah, these folks have been through the wringer. They know their stuff, and they're ready to do what's necessary," Clay replied, his tone serious yet optimistic. "We're all here for the same reason—to secure a future where nights like these are about peace, not war prep."

As we continued our walk through the camp, we stopped by the central command tent where maps and satellite images were laid out. Officers and strategists from different factions were deep in discussion, pointing at routes and potential conflict zones.

"Seeing all this," I gestured to the maps and the bustling camp, "reminds me how much we've come together. It's not just about fighting; it's about building something that lasts beyond the battles."

Clay nodded, "Exactly. We're not just patching holes; we're laying new foundations. But remember, this operation is just the start. We've got to be ready for the long haul."

The preparations continued into the night, with briefings and equipment checks ensuring that everyone was ready. As I looked around, I saw faces determined and resolute, bolstered by the presence of seasoned leaders like Clay.

"Let's make sure we do this right," I said to Clay as we concluded our inspection of the artillery units. "Not just for us, but for the generations that will hear about what we did here and build on it."

Clay clasped my shoulder firmly, "We'll do it right, or we won't do it at all. That's the promise we're making here tonight."

As night fully settled over Farm Bridge, the campfires flickered like stars against the dark landscape, a small reflection of the hope and fire within us all. Tomorrow, we would march east, toward uncertainty and conflict, but tonight, we were united in our resolve to fight for a future worth living.

The March Begins

As the dawn broke over Farm Bridge, the crisp air was filled with the mixed emotions of anticipation and apprehension. Today was the day we were set to march, a moment we had all been preparing for but none had eagerly awaited. The camp was bustling with activity; soldiers checking their gear, saying their goodbyes, and lining up in formation.

I walked among the troops, offering words of encouragement and sharing in the solemn mood that had blanketed the camp. Lucky trotted alongside me, his presence a comforting constant in the sea of change. Every now and then, he would stop to sniff at the soldiers' bags, perhaps hoping to understand why there was so much commotion.

Robbie stood at the edge of the formation, his expression torn between a desire to join and his duty to stay. His sister, standing beside him, held his hand tightly, offering silent support. It was a poignant reminder of the personal sacrifices everyone in the camp was grappling with.

As I approached the front of the line, Ruslana was overseeing the final preparations. Her face was set in determination, each decision weighed with the gravity of the lives it impacted. She caught my eye and nodded, a silent acknowledgment of the burden we both shared.

"Let's keep the lines tight and maintain communication at all times," Ruslana instructed her officers. Her voice was firm, cutting through the morning air with precision.

Turning to me, she said, "It's a crucial moment for the Republic.

We need to ensure our forces are not just brave but also smart. We can't afford reckless bravery."

I nodded in agreement, knowing that the success of this mission would define the future of the newly formed Republic. The troops began to march, their steps synchronized, as they moved past the gates of Farm Bridge and into the uncertain landscape beyond.

Lucky barked, running up to the front of the column before returning to my side, as if making sure I was still following. I patted his head, grateful for his loyal company.

The day progressed with the slow rhythm of a marching army. The landscape around us gradually shifted from the familiar sights of Farm Bridge to the more desolate expanses that marked the territories still recovering from the war's devastation.

As we set up camp for the night, the fatigue of the day's march was visible on everyone's faces, but so was a sense of purpose. We gathered around the campfires, sharing meals and stories, the glow of the firelight casting dancing shadows on thoughtful faces.

I sat with a small group, including Clay and his girlfriend, discussing the logistics of the upcoming days and the strategies we would employ. The conversation was technical but necessary, grounding us in the reality of our mission amidst the swirling emotions of departure.

Tonight, under the vast starlit sky, we were not just soldiers or survivors but a community united by a common goal—to secure a future worth fighting for. As I looked around at the gathered faces illuminated by the firelight, I felt a renewed sense of commitment to our cause, bolstered by the bonds that tie us together.

Tomorrow would bring more marching, more challenges, but for tonight, we rested, ready to face whatever lay ahead.

The March of the California Republic

The morning was crisp as 1,058 combat-ready troops, dressed in U.S. military fatigues, lined up in formation. These weren't just any clothes; they were a symbol of unity, provided by Clay's group. We were transforming from a collective of survivors into a structured military force, a physical representation of what the President had called "Nation Builders." This new identity was crucial—not just for morale but for the vision we were trying to achieve. The California Republic was not just surviving; it was asserting itself on a larger stage.

Emotions ran high as we prepared to depart. Clara and Watson shared a poignant moment, reminiscent of a scene from another era—a knight going off to battle with a token from his lady. She handed him a lock of her hair, which he reverently kissed before tucking it away. This small act was a powerful reminder of the personal stakes involved in our mission.

Next to them, I held Alexis close, memorizing everything about her—her scent, the feel of her hair, the warmth of her body. It was a moment of deep personal significance, knowing what lay ahead and what I was leaving behind. Beside us, Annie tried to console a visibly distraught Lilith, whose emotions overflowed in contrast to the stoic demeanor most of us maintained.

Saying goodbye to Robbie and Meg was equally tough. Robbie wished me luck with a firm handshake that spoke volumes of the gravity of our departure. Turning to join the march, I felt the weight of responsibility on my shoulders—not just as a soldier but as someone who had seen too much and feared what more he might see.

Our battalion was organized into three companies, each supported by a heavy weapons platoon. This included two Strikers and two additional armored vehicles for support—key assets given the potential threats we faced. As we marched, I thought about the future and the past, the place at Big Bear where we might one day settle down, and the silent, insidious threat of the Fuego, burning ever more insistently in the back of my mind.

Our journey east was not just a physical trek but a passage through our hopes and fears, each step a move towards a potential new beginning or a devastating loss. The rhythm of marching feet and the steady cadence of military chants helped focus our minds on the task ahead, but the shadows of what we had left behind and what we were marching towards loomed large over us all.

Ruslana met us outside the perimeter of our camp, where the faint glow of moon and stars penetrated the lingering clouds, casting a dim light on our discussion. Watson and I had requested this meeting to discuss a temporary but crucial departure from the main force.

"We need to leave for a few days," I began, keeping my voice low to avoid being overheard by nearby sentries. "We've identified a potential strategic opportunity that could give us an edge, but it requires our personal attention."

Ruslana, looking every bit the leader in her pragmatic military gear, nodded thoughtfully. "Where are you headed?" she asked, her tone conveying both concern and trust.

"We can't disclose the exact location yet, not until we've confirmed a few things. It's a sensitive operation," Watson added, his expression serious. The gruffness in his voice matched the severity of our plan.

Ruslana's eyes narrowed slightly, assessing the sincerity and urgency of our request. After a moment, she responded, "Alright. I trust your judgment. But keep your communicators on and check in daily. If anything changes here, you'll need to come back immediately."

"We understand," I replied, feeling the weight of her trust. "We'll maintain radio silence unless absolutely necessary to ensure security."

With a final nod, Ruslana turned back towards the camp, her figure blending into the shadows cast by the flickering light of distant campfires. Watson and I then prepared for our departure, gathering the necessary gear for our reconnaissance mission.

Our goal was clear, though fraught with risks. We aimed to scout an area rumored to hold a significant tactical advantage. Success could shift the balance in our favor, but failure could expose us to new threats. As we slipped away from the camp, the silent night seemed to hold its breath, the stars above watching silently as we ventured into the uncertain darkness.

A Covert Mission

Ruslana took a deep breath, the weight of command evident in her furrowed brow. "I can't be involved in this officially. Whatever you do out there, it's not under the banner of the California Republic."

Watson and I nodded in understanding. We were about to undertake a mission that could easily blur the lines between necessity and morality, potentially tipping the scales of our nascent government's legitimacy.

"I know," I replied. "This is off the books. We'll handle it discreetly and only intervene if absolutely necessary. Our goal is to confirm the threat, not engage unless we have no other choice."

Ruslana looked between us, her expression hardening with resolve. "Be careful. If this goes south, it could jeopardize everything we've built. You're not just scouts now; you're guardians of this republic, in more ways than one."

"We understand the stakes," Watson added, his voice firm. "We'll use minimal force and maximum stealth. We'll avoid contact and focus on gathering intelligence."

Ruslana gave us a final nod, the unspoken gravity of the situation hanging between us like the cold night air. "Check in every 12 hours. If I don't hear from you, I'll assume the worst."

We packed our gear, ensuring we carried only what was necessary to avoid drawing attention. The night was quiet as we set out, the faint sounds of the camp fading behind us. Our steps were light, our presence minimal as we moved through the shadows, blending into the landscape that was all too familiar yet unpredictably dangerous.

Watson and I headed straight for Havasu City, using our knowledge of the area and our low profiles to navigate through the dangerous landscape. The city had become a hub of activity under the Iron Lady's rule, and if there were any reserve forces or plans against the California Republic, they would likely be coordinated there.

As we moved closer to the city, the reality of our mission weighed heavily on us. We weren't just scouting; we were potentially setting the stage for a confrontation that could decide the fate of many. It was imperative that we gathered accurate intelligence without drawing attention to ourselves.

The south end of Lake Havasu was particularly strategic, not just for its water resources but also for the livestock pens located there. These pens were crucial for feeding the army of the dawn, and the Colorado River's outflow provided a natural barrier, making it a defensive stronghold.

Our approach was methodical. We avoided main roads, using lesser-known trails and occasionally blending in with local traffic. Every checkpoint was a risk, but being recognized occasionally actually helped rather than hindered, providing a cover for our real intentions.

Once we reached the outskirts of Havasu City, we planned to observe military movements and supply routes. The location was perfect for monitoring without being too conspicuous. If the Iron Lady had indeed gathered a reserve force, there would be signs of it here—increased military activity, new encampments, or stockpiling of resources.

Our mission was clear: confirm the presence of any reserve force and understand its capabilities. Any findings would be critical for the California Republic's strategic planning. The next few days would require all our focus and stealth, as we delved deeper into enemy territory, ever aware of the delicate balance of power that could shift with the information we gathered.

Watson and I managed to isolate a slave working on the animal side of the butchery. The whole setup was depressingly efficient, designed to maximize the use of every resource, including human lives. The man we cornered looked like he could have been anyone's neighbor before the world fell apart—now, just another face among the oppressed, his eyes filled with the resigned fear of the downtrodden.

In the shadowy confines of a work shack, I spoke in low, even tones to keep the conversation private and to avoid alarming him further. "Listen, I'm not here to hurt you. But I need information, and if you help me, I'll make sure you're okay. I need to know about the shipments—specifically, anything headed east. What can you tell me?"

His initial hesitation was palpable, the result of countless abuses no doubt, but the promise of safety seemed to ease his tension slightly. He glanced around nervously before responding in a hushed tone, ensuring no overseers were nearby to overhear us.

"They ship out once every week, early in the morning before most are awake. Trucks—lots of them—full of supplies. Food, mostly, but sometimes boxes that are guarded more heavily. Those go directly to the army, not for the pens. They head east, towards the front lines."

I pressed further, "Do you know where exactly these shipments are going? Any specific locations or is it all just general supply runs?"

He shook his head, a mixture of fear and ignorance clear in his expression. "No, sir, just east. They keep it quiet, but sometimes you hear things. There's talk of a big push, gathering more troops. Heard some guards saying it's going to be a major operation."

This was the piece of intelligence we needed. A major operation could imply a concentration of forces or a significant military undertaking. Watson, who had been silently observing, finally spoke up, his voice low and urgent. "We need to find out where these troops are gathering. It's crucial we understand their strength and the scale of this operation."

Thanking the slave, I reassured him of his safety and quickly moved away with Watson to discuss our next steps. This information pointed to a potential buildup of forces by the Iron Lady, possibly preparing for a significant offensive. Our next move would be to trace these supply routes eastward, towards the front lines, to gather more precise details on the troop movements and their ultimate objective.

As we exited the shack, blending back into the grim daily life of the butchery, the weight of our discovery hung heavily between us. We needed to move quickly and carefully, understanding that each piece of information we gathered could significantly alter the balance of power in the ongoing conflict.

A Sudden Confrontation

The foreman had barged into the shack, club in hand, with an angry glare. His accusation was loud, but the fire in my brain drowned out his voice. He recognized me, and that recognition carried a mix of fear and fury. He didn't have time to process what was happening before my fist connected with his jaw, catching him off guard.

His surprise staggered him backward, and I followed through with a swift knee to his gut. The club slipped from his grasp, clattering to the ground as he doubled over in pain. His breath came out in gasps, and his eyes widened as he looked up at me, realizing his mistake.

In a flash, I snatched the club from the ground and brought it down, aiming to incapacitate, not to kill. A solid thud echoed in the shack as the wood struck the back of his legs, and he crumpled to the floor, wincing in pain. Watson, stoic as ever, watched with a stony expression, ready to jump in if needed but understanding the need to handle this quietly.

The slave watched us with wide eyes, fear etched across his features as he scrambled backward, seeking refuge in the shadowy corners of the shack. I met his gaze and motioned for him to stay quiet. He nodded vigorously, clutching his knees to his chest as he huddled against the wall.

I crouched beside the foreman, his groans the only sound breaking the heavy silence. "You're going to forget you saw us here. You're going to pretend this didn't happen and go back to your miserable life. Understand?"

His breath was labored, but he nodded, grimacing from the pain in his abdomen. "Y-Yes," he wheezed, his voice barely a whisper.

I glanced at Watson, who gave a curt nod. We had what we needed, and it was time to move before anyone else showed up. I turned back to the foreman, "Good. Remember, we're just ghosts. Now get out of here."

He crawled toward the door, using the frame to pull himself up before staggering away, his gait unsteady. We turned our attention back to the slave, who still cowered in the shadows. I leaned down, voice low and steady, "Go back to your work. Don't mention us. Your silence is the best way to survive here."

He nodded frantically again, scrambling up to his feet and

backing out of the shack without a word. Watson and I exchanged one last glance before slipping back into the grim daily life of the butchery, blending with the workers as we made our way out.

We now had a direction: North. The Iron Lady was gathering forces up there, and our mission was to find out why. With that knowledge, we slipped into the shadows, heading towards the outskirts of the butchery to track down the trail leading northward.

After Watson's stark warning, we walked on in heavy silence, each step echoing the grim reality of my situation. The desert around us was quiet, too quiet, as if it held its breath, watching the drama of human struggles unfold amidst its timeless sands.

"We need to focus on the task at hand," Watson finally said, breaking the silence. His voice was firm, a reminder of the mission that lay ahead of us. "We got to figure out where these reserves are and what The Iron Lady is really planning. This isn't just about your condition, it's about what's best for everyone back home."

I nodded, feeling the weight of responsibility tighten around my shoulders. "You're right. Let's keep moving north. If there's a reserve force, we'll find it."

The landscape was rugged, scattered with the ruins of what once might have been a thriving area. Now, it was just another part of the vast wasteland, marked by the scars of war and neglect. The occasional rusted car or crumbling building served as a stark reminder of the world that had been lost.

As we advanced, I kept replaying the encounter in the pen, the violence that had erupted so quickly. It was a clear sign that the Fuego was a more formidable enemy than I had admitted. "Watson," I started, hesitantly, "if it comes down to it, if I start losing it, you have to take me out. Promise me that."

Watson didn't look at me, his eyes fixed on the horizon, scanning for any signs of trouble. "You don't have to ask. But let's make sure it doesn't come to that. Keep fighting it, and use that fire for something good."

We set up a temporary camp as night began to fall, not daring to light a fire that could attract unwanted attention. Instead, we sat under the cold glow of the stars, each lost in our own thoughts but united by a common goal.

The next day, we continued northward, determined to uncover the truth behind The Iron Lady's mysterious losses and the whereabouts of the alleged reserve force. Each step was a test of will, a balance between the need to push forward and the threat that simmered within me, a constant reminder of the dual battles I faced: one against the external enemies and one against the darkness within.

A Risky Plan Takes Shape

As the night enveloped our camp with its oppressive darkness, Ruslana huddled with her commanders and Annie to discuss the precarious situation we found ourselves in. The Iron Lady's territory, while secured, posed a significant threat due to its stability and strict surveillance. Yet, her military prowess was a double-edged sword; it offered us a clear and vital pathway to strike but left little room for error.

"Our focus must remain sharp," Ruslana began, her voice low but filled with a resolute strength. "We can't just retreat now without consequences. We need a solid strategy that ensures we don't escalate this into an open conflict with The Iron Lady."

Annie, always meticulous with details, laid out the logistics. "The supply routes are our best option. They are well-guarded, but they also offer a potential weak point. If we can disguise ourselves within these operations, we might be able to infiltrate deeper into enemy lines."

The plan was daring. We would use the regularity of the supply convoys to blend in, moving stealthily towards the front lines. Once there, it would be up to me to find a moment when The Iron Lady was less guarded, a moment of vulnerability.

"Remember, the aim is not just to confront her," Ruslana reminded everyone. "We need to understand her next moves, assess her strength, and if possible, neutralize her capacity to strike back at the Republic."

The weight of this responsibility was not lost on me. My proximity to The Iron Lady during my time in her territory had given me insights into her operations, but this familiarity also painted a large target on my back. If recognized, it could unravel the entire operation.

"We'll need to disguise you," one of the commanders suggested. "Change your appearance, maybe alter the way you carry yourself. Anything that can help you blend in better."

Annie nodded in agreement. "We'll also need a contingency plan. If things go south, we need a way out that doesn't lead straight to a slaughter."

The discussion continued into the early hours, with every detail scrutinized and every potential outcome considered. The tension was palpable; we all understood the stakes were incredibly high—not just for us personally but for the future of the Republic.

As the meeting adjourned, Ruslana pulled me aside. "I know this is a lot to ask, but you're the only one with the unique insights and experience to pull this off. We all trust you."

With a heavy heart, I prepared myself mentally for the days ahead. The plan was set, and soon, I would find myself face to face with The Iron Lady once again. This time, however, the encounter wouldn't just determine my fate, but potentially the fate of the entire Republic.

Tense Moments at the Front

Annie and I navigated through a sprawling field hospital, our senses overwhelmed by the sight of wounded soldiers and the pervasive scent of antiseptics and blood. It was a grim reminder of the costs of war, a stark contrast to the organized chaos that defined the command areas.

The Iron Lady's command post was fortified impressively, with deep trenches encircling it, reflecting her heightened paranoia and strategic foresight following past close calls with death. As we approached the makeshift moat, I was struck by the meticulousness of her defenses, a sign of her unwavering resolve to maintain control no matter the cost.

Crossing the wooden bridge felt symbolic, like stepping into the lion's den, and as we emerged on the other side, The Iron Lady awaited us, her presence as commanding as ever. Despite the dirt and disorder of the battlefield, she was pristine in her military garb, each medal and insignia polished to a shine.

"Your timing is impeccable," she greeted us, her voice carrying the weight of command yet tinged with a trace of genuine relief, perhaps pleased to see familiar faces amid the turmoil.

She led us into her tent, which served as her mobile headquarters. Inside, the stark military efficiency continued, with maps and communication equipment meticulously arranged. Her focus was absolute, her energy directed at managing the ongoing conflict and planning the next moves against the Aztecos.

Despite the chaos outside, inside the tent, there was a palpable sense of order. It was clear she thrived in this environment, each challenge and setback only sharpening her resolve.

Annie remained quiet, her thoughts obviously elsewhere, likely wrestling with the moral complexities of our mission and what it might mean for the future of the Republic. Her silence was heavy with unspoken concerns, reflecting the inner conflict faced by many who found themselves fighting in a war where the lines between right and wrong were blurred.

The meeting with The Iron Lady was brief. She updated us on the status of the front lines, discussed logistical challenges, and shared her strategic plans for the coming days. It was all business; every decision and order calculated to achieve maximum impact with minimal loss, at least for her forces.

As we left the command tent, the weight of the situation settled on my shoulders like a lead cloak. The reality of war, with its stark brutality and complex moral entanglements, was overwhelming. Yet, amidst it all, there was a clarity in The Iron Lady's approach that demanded a certain respect, even if it couldn't be fully endorsed.

Annie and I walked back through the medical tents in silence, each lost in our thoughts. The path ahead was fraught with danger, not just from the enemy, but from the decisions we would have to make, decisions that could alter the course of the war and the lives of all those involved.

The Iron Lady and I stood over her map table, discussing the daunting situation on the front lines. Her confession about the sheer number of Aztecos pressing against her positions had taken me by surprise. "30 to 50 thousand at the start," she reiterated, her voice steady despite the staggering numbers.

"They threw waves of fighters at us relentlessly," she continued, marking previous positions on the map where her forces had been overwhelmed. "We've been forced to retreat multiple times. This spot here," she pointed to a marked area on the map, "is our fifth fallback position."

I absorbed the information, trying to hide my shock. The Iron Lady seemed composed, almost resigned to the brutal reality of her situation. "It's been a war of attrition, and we're bleeding more than we can sustain. That's why your forces are so crucial right now."

She moved a few pieces on the map, illustrating the strategic placement of the Republic's forces on the southern flank. "We expect the next major assault to hit here," she indicated, her finger pressing firmly on a critical junction. "Your troops will need to hold this line. It's vital."

The gravity of the situation settled heavily between us. The responsibility of commanding a crucial section of the front was daunting, but necessary. "We're ready," I assured her, my voice firm. "We'll hold the line."

The Iron Lady nodded, a hint of relief in her expression. "I know you will. I wouldn't have agreed to this position if I didn't believe in your troops' capability."

As the meeting wrapped up, she stood and extended her hand, a gesture of formal solidarity. "Good luck," she said, her gaze intense but weary.

I shook her hand, feeling the weight of the coming days. As I left the tent, the scale of the challenge ahead was clear. The Republic's forces were about to face the fiercest fighting yet, and everything hinged on our ability to stand firm.

The Iron Lady's offer echoed in my mind, unsettling yet strangely compelling. Her knowledge of my condition, the Fuego's effects on me, and her straightforward proposition revealed a depth of insight and preparation I hadn't fully appreciated before. Her proposal wasn't just an escape; it was a calculated recruitment based on very personal leverage.

"You know the state I'm in," I started slowly, grappling with the gravity of her offer. "You think I'd be of any use to you in this condition?"

"More than you know," Evan replied, her tone serious. "You've seen firsthand what we're up against. Your experience, your... condition... it gives you insights none of my men can match."

I pondered her words, the temptation of a safe haven for Alexis and my friends gnawing at my conscience. "And what about the people at Farm Bridge? What happens to the Republic if I just walk away?"

The Iron Lady leaned back slightly, her expression hardening with strategic calculation. "The Republic will survive, or it won't. That's on them, not you. You need to think about your immediate circle, about Alexis. You said it yourself, you're a ticking time bomb. Why not use the time you have left for something… bigger?"

Her argument was cold, logical, brutally pragmatic—hallmarks of her leadership style. But it also made an uncomfortable amount of sense. Still, the thought of abandoning the larger fight, of walking away from a community I helped to build, weighed heavily on me.

"What if I said I need some time to think about it?" I asked, trying to buy some space to breathe, to think.

"You have until we break camp at dawn. After that, we're moving out, and the offer is off the table," she stated flatly, a finality in her voice that expected no further debate.

I nodded slowly, the decision looming over me like a dark cloud. As I walked away from the tent, the distant sounds of war mixed with the restless thoughts swirling in my head. Defecting could mean safety, a chance to use my remaining days to fight on my terms. But at what cost? Loyalty, integrity, and perhaps a piece of my soul.

That night, sleep was elusive. Every time I closed my eyes, I saw the faces of my friends, of Alexis, and the life we might secure if I accepted The Iron Lady's offer. Yet, each imagined scenario played out like a betrayal, a surrender of everything we had fought for. By dawn, my decision was clear, though not any easier for its clarity.

The Onset of Battle

The battlefield was silent for a breath holding moment as anticipation hung thick in the air. The seasoned soldier's radio crackled back to life, confirming the order had been received. His eyes were fixed on the horizon, where the faint outlines of the frenzied Azteco horde began to take shape against the dark sky.

"Fire in the hole!" came the shout, a split second before the ground itself seemed to roar to life. From our position, I could see the front lines of the Republic's defenses light up as multiple artillery units opened fire. The night was shattered by the deafening booms of heavy artillery, each blast sending shockwaves through the air and into our bones.

As the shells arced overhead, brilliant explosions blossomed across the no-man's land where the horde advanced. Each explosion was a deadly flower of light and shrapnel, tearing through the ranks of the Aztecos with ruthless efficiency. The sound was overwhelming, a relentless thunder that echoed off the surrounding hills.

Beside me, Ruslana's face was a mask of grim determination. She knew the cost of each shell, the price of the firepower needed to hold back the tide. Her jaw was set, her eyes tracking the impact of each explosion, calculating the effectiveness of their placement.

The Iron Lady, ever the strategist, watched the unfolding chaos with a critical eye. Her lips moved silently, likely counting the seconds between barrages, assessing the enemy's momentum. Her hands were clasped behind her back, her posture rigid against the backdrop of war.

The horde's advance was momentarily halted by the barrage, but only momentarily. They were too many, too frenzied to be deterred by fear or loss. As the artillery's roar tapered off, the eerie sound of their war drums filled the air again, a sinister reminder that this was just the beginning.

"Prepare for close combat!" shouted the seasoned soldier, turning to relay further commands through his radio. The Republic's troops braced themselves, checking their weapons and steeling their nerves for the chaos to come.

As the first of the Aztecos reached the outer defenses, the night erupted into smaller, more personal battles. The sound of gunfire joined the symphony of war, a staccato counterpoint to the ongoing drumming of the horde.

Next to me, Watson's hand found the butt of his rifle, his expression one of resolve mixed with a hint of resignation. He knew, as did I, that the night would be long and the fighting brutal. Annie stood close by, her rifle already raised, her eyes scanning for the first targets to come into view.

This was war, unfiltered and savage, and as the two forces collided with the ferocity of ancient enemies, the air was filled with the cries of the wounded, the roar of guns, and the relentless drumbeat of an enemy that knew no fear.

As the night turned into a canvas of fire and smoke, the relentless advance of the Aztecos seemed almost supernatural. Each burst of artillery and the accompanying shower of tracers illuminated the battlefield, revealing the horrific resolve of the horde. The ground was littered with the fallen, yet for every Azteco that fell, more surged forward, undeterred by the hail of lead and steel.

Our heavy weapons continued to roar, each round designed to halt the advance of the enemy. The noise was deafening, a constant thunder that vibrated in the chest and rattled the teeth. Above the din, the shouts of our commanders could be heard, directing the fire and maneuvering troops to plug the gaps in our lines.

The Aztecos, fueled by Fuego, seemed immune to fear or pain. Their charge was relentless, a tidal wave of flesh and fury that sought to overwhelm through sheer force of numbers. Our defenses held, but it was clear that this was a battle of attrition we were ill-prepared to sustain for long.

From my position next to Ruslana and The Iron Lady, I could see the strain on the commanders' faces. Each one knew the stakes; each one understood that if our lines broke, the consequences would be catastrophic. Ruslana's voice was hoarse from shouting orders, her face set in a grim line of determination. Beside her, The Iron Lady watched the battle unfold with an icy calm, her mind no doubt calculating the cost of each life spent in defense of her realm.

The mortars continued their deadly ballet, sending more anti-personnel rounds screaming into the enemy ranks. The ground shook with each impact, a grim drumbeat to the chaos of battle. The air was thick with the smell of gunpowder and blood, a pungent reminder of the violence that enveloped us.

In the midst of this maelstrom, I felt a cold clarity settle over me. This was what the Fuego had prepared me for: a fight not just for survival, but for the very soul of our new world. I knew that in the hours to come, I would be tested as never before. As I clutched my rifle and prepared to join the fray, I couldn't help but think of Alexis and the promise I had made to her. The promise to return.

With a deep breath, I stepped forward, ready to meet whatever came next, determined to fight not just for survival, but for a future worth living in. The battle raged on, and I was one with it, another soldier in a war that would decide the fate of nations.

CONCLUSION

Aftermath and Reflections

As The Iron Lady scrubbed the night from her face, the weight of command etched deep into her features, she continued speaking. "We wouldn't have stood a chance holding off another attack if it weren't for your reinforcements. The firepower your people brought made all the difference tonight."

I leaned against the tent's support, watching her. Every splash of water seemed to wash away a layer of the battlefield's dust and blood, but not the underlying tension that clung to her like a second skin.

She paused, catching her reflection in a small mirror propped against the tent wall. "It's a temporary reprieve, though," she added, her voice dropping to a near whisper. "They'll regroup and come at us harder and more prepared next time."

I nodded, understanding the cyclical nature of warfare all too well. "We need to use this time wisely, then. Boost our defenses, maybe push forward while they're licking their wounds."

She straightened up, turning to face me fully, a hint of appreciation in her eyes. "Exactly. We push them back, harry their flanks, do whatever we can to keep them off balance. Your troops are disciplined, well-equipped. It's more than I hoped for."

The conversation shifted as she dried her face, her demeanor hardening once again. "But let's not kid ourselves. This war is far from over. I need your forces ready to move out as soon as we've reorganized. Can I count on you for that?"

Her question hung in the air, a test of commitment and resolve. I felt the weight of her gaze, measuring my response before I'd even voiced it.

"You can," I affirmed, feeling the resolve of steel within me. "We'll be ready. Whatever it takes to end this."

The Iron Lady nodded, a rare smile flickering across her face. "Good. Get some rest now. We'll need every ounce of strength for what's coming."

As I exited the tent, the first light of dawn painted the sky a pale blue, a stark contrast to the night's horrors. The air was still filled with the smell of gunpowder and blood, but beneath it all, there was a faint hint of possibility. A chance to turn the tide in a war that had seemed unwinnable just days before.

As the camp erupted into chaos with the fall of The Iron Lady, emotions swirled like a storm. The warriors and commanders, caught between shock and rage, struggled to grasp the sudden power vacuum. My proclamation that Azteco assassins were responsible turned their grief into a blind fury directed outward, away from introspection and potential infighting that could tear them apart.

Stepping forward, I addressed the assembled masses, my voice carrying over the din. "This is what they do! The aztecos aim to destroy what we have built by taking our leader! We must unite, or we fall divided and weak!"

Confusion and anger mingled in the air as her loyalists grappled with their loss. I saw groups of soldiers clenching their fists, their faces hardening with resolve. They needed direction, and I provided it with a call to honor The Iron Lady's legacy by continuing the fight.

"We will not let her vision die here! We march not just for revenge, but to secure our future! For The Iron Lady!" The response was a thunderous roar of approval. It wasn't just about avenging a leader but preserving the stability she had enforced with an iron fist.

The commanders, now looking to me for leadership, gathered to quickly discuss the next steps. We needed to maintain order within the ranks and ensure that the aztecos couldn't exploit our moment of weakness.

As the meeting unfolded, we planned a retaliatory strike against the azteco forces. It was crucial to demonstrate strength quickly to prevent any thoughts of dissent or defection among the troops. "Prepare the men," I instructed the nearest commander. "We strike at dawn. Let the aztecos feel the wrath they have invoked."

The rest of the day was a blur of preparations. Armor was repaired, weapons were distributed, and the wounded were tended to with a renewed sense of urgency. The camp transformed from a place of mourning to a hive of military efficiency, all geared towards a singular goal: a crushing blow against our enemies.

That night, as I lay in my tent, the weight of the day's events pressed heavily upon me. The Iron Lady's final words echoed in my mind, a grim reminder of the brutal necessities of leadership in such dire times. The path forward was fraught with peril, but it was a path we had to walk. For her, for us, for the fragile semblance of civilization we clung to in this chaotic new world.

"Stay tuned for the next part of this saga, where the battle continues, alliances are tested, and new heroes rise from the ashes of the old world. The journey is not yet complete, and the fight for the future is just beginning."

◆ ◆ ◆

www.ingramcontent.com/pod-product-compliance
Lightning Source LLC
Chambersburg PA
CBHW051552250726
48653CB00004BA/1118